Retrogrades

Mohan Koparkar Ph.D.

Copyright 1980
Mohan Koparkar
Mohan Enterprises
P.O. Box 8334
Roch., N.Y. 14618

Table of Contents

Introduction
General descriptions, Retrogrades and House rulerships, Retrogrades and Interceptions, Retrograde in Groups, progressions, transits, Reincarnation, and in Mundane Astrology   **5**

Retrograde Mercury
Through the houses, ruling the houses, opposite all the direct planets, opposite all the retrograde planets   **15**

Retrograde Venus
Through the houses, ruling the houses, opposite all the direct planets, opposite all the retrograde planets   **33**

Retrograde Mars
Through the houses, ruling the houses, opposite all the direct planets   **52**

Retrograde Jupiter
Through the houses, ruling the houses, opposite all the direct planets   **68**

Retrograde Saturn
Through the houses, ruling the houses, opposite all the direct planets   **83**

Retrograde Uranus
Through the houses, ruling the houses, opposite all the direct planets   **98**

Retrograde Neptune
Through the houses, ruling the houses, opposite all the direct planets   **112**

Retrograde Pluto
Through the houses, ruling the houses, opposite all the direct planets   **127**

INTRODUCTION

The retrogradation is a phenomenon of the opposition. When an orbit of earth positions in such a way to be in the middle of an inner and an outer planet, the relative motion of one of them appears in the opposite direction to that of the other. This also occurs due to velocity variation in the planets within the orbit of earth. Consequently, we on earth observe a motion of the planet that is opposite in direction to our standardized planetary movement. All the planets in the solar system undergo this reversal imagery except the Sun and the Moon. The retrogradation is a relative phenomenon that describes the path of growth in native in nonsequential form. The programming sequence of a standard planet upon a newly born person follows certain procedures. However, a retrograde motion that is an apparent reverse motion with respect to earth may indicate unconventional variation of its qualities. As a result, a retrograde planet will implant its seeds of qualities which may differ in growth and reactions as the native evolves in life. For deeper influence, a retrograde planet should remain the same for few of the early days after birth. A planet that changes direction right after birth and goes direct will have a least impact upon that native by virtue of its retrogradation. The retrograde planet has a capability to totally change its perspectives and normal behavior within limits. Although it cannot defy its character, it tries hard to be most flexible and adaptable with others. This adaptability and ability to switch hats, leaves him with lesser priorities over other planets. His qualities are often subdued at times and compromised to the other governing planets. The governing planets are the heavenly bodies which become responsible for its retrograde motion. Thus, a retrograde planet will have three possible combinations:

1. Retrograde position with no oppositions to it.
2. Retrograde position with an opposition to a direct planet.
3. Retrograde position with an opposition to another retrograde planet.

Since the retrograde motion exhibits adaptability and compromise, it will be forced to do so to its master who forms the opposition. In case of no opposition to the retrograde planet, individual freedom and adaptability are at its own will. Thus a planet with no opposition in retrogradation will be his own boss dictating the self-discipline of individual freedom as he pleases. This freedom of choice will display a wide variation in the qualities without strict restrictions controlled by any outside force. The planet does not have to abide by any rules and regulations except its own. The free floating attitude will precipitate such a quality in the programming of that native.

When in opposition, the retrograde planet will have to abide by and compromise to the planet in opposition. Here the retrograde planet accepts the inferiorty temporarily by allowing the other planet the right of way. This compromise or temporary retreat is done as the planet is not sure of its potential and growth direction. It takes time to evaluate his long term strategies under such conflicting situations. This adaptability is not forced upon him but it is an internal protecting mechanism to preserve his longevity. It is best to assess the enemy strength than create an all out attack in this war of opposition. In doing so, the native feels frustrated regarding the qualities of the retrograde planets. Minor inadequecies sink-in and fear of lack of power felt. However, these judgements and self evaluating techniques are important in the esoteric learnings of life. As a result of this, delineations of the retrograde planets appear pessimistic or negative. This is to understand the human impotency when something does not react, does not mean it is nonaggressive. The nonaggression policy helps maintain adequate peace within that individual by way of self-created compromises. The side effect of this give-in tendency may be too much of a retreat in certain areas of life which the person has to suffer. However, these learning lessons are a must for his growth. Unless he learns to accept that, his spiritual and material growth is hampered due to inner self destruction. When in opposition, a retrograde planet encounters another retrograde planet, the situation can be very tense and volatile. This only occurs with one inner planet such as Mercury or Venus and any other planets beyond earth. In doing this stand-out situation, internal or personal planets clash with external or impersonal planets. At this turning point, both planets have to learn to abide by and compromise to the other planet. Learning to coexist, using the available weaponry can be difficult in the life of that individual. Compromises are working for cross purposes and there may not be any independent judge to evaluate mutual participation. The balance is achieved in the qualities of those planets in that opposition by their own willingness. Unique phenomenon of a stronger planet giving priority to a weaker one is seen here. In doing so, it respects another's superiority and strength no matter at what level it can be. This compromise hurts the native more than the planetary egos. The native has to adjust his personality and capability of the planetary power in view of this tug of wars. Inferiorities gather within, hostilities buildup and nervous stresses exceed the anticipated levels in this case. Here external calm does not justify internal anguish. The native tries to push himself hard towards achievements, but inner friction and impedence from inertia oppose him greatly. The outcome appears as an inefficient usage of planetary energies and the native runs around in circles making the same mistakes. The repetition of circumstances and reactions to the same situations help him achieve better status eventually on the Karmic ladder. The learning and relearning experiences seem redundant to him, but not to the "Guy" up there who thrives on perfection of human soul.

Introduction

In summary regarding the usage of this text, locate the planets that are retrograde in the chart.
- Determine if a retrograde planet is without any opposition using as wide an orb as 8°. For a retrograde planet without any opposition read the description at the appropriate place.
- If a retrograde planet is opposite a planet that is direct in motion, you find that combination, such as Retrograde Mercury opposite Mars.
- If a retrograde planet is opposite a planet that is also retrograde, look for appropriate section, such as Retrograde Mercury opposite retrograde Mars.
- If a retrograde planet is opposite several of the planets, then study each opposition separately. In that case, its compromises are shared towards those planets and the separate descriptions should be mellowed appropriately. If the group that is opposite a retrograde planet contains a planet that is retrograde, then that planet will be much weaker, subdued or diffused in its nature. Here that planet compromises to all direct planets involved in the vicinity by way of a catalyst of the retrograde planet in opposition. Usually a retrograde planet conjunct a regular planet will not be as weak unless there is an opposition to the combination. Basically, an opposition is making the retrograde planet retreat slightly to start with. This also gives an opportunity for rebellion and retaliation. Most frustrative effects or outcomes upon the native come from this rebellious retaliation by a retrograde planet when he least expects it.
- All other aspects to retrograde planets are treated as usual without regard for compromising or adaptable treatments.
- After studying the retrograde planet in any one of the above three major categories, its house rulership will be of great essence. Thus, for Retrograde Mercury, read the sections where the signs Gemini and Virgo are ruling the houses in that chart. e.g. Retrograde Mercury in a chart with Virgo rising and Gemini on the mid-heaven, read the description under: Retrograde Mercury ruling the 10th and the 1st house.
- The house occupied by a retrograde planet will be studied next. Due to its indecisive, flexible and adaptable nature, the retrograde planet creates diffused qualities in that house. Thus, rather than being a defined self-image, one notices a blurry identity in that house. As a result, the qualities of the retrograde planet in a house will be much weaker, insecure, and uncertain of its purpose. To over compensate for this image, the retrograde planet will display periodic explosive rebellion. This accounts for the delineations under this section more pessimistic or difficult in nature. Keep in mind that they not only occur abruptly but with sudden intensity. Under usual conditions, this planet will be well behaved and "chart trained". Doing something different from normal will be its basic goal. The distortions or abnormalities are just to get the attention from that soul regarding those learning experiences. Knowing this will be a partial relief to the reader who would find this section less frustrating and critical regarding the analyses.

RETROGRADE UNDERSTANDING THROUGH THE HOUSE RULERSHIP

As mentioned before regarding the compromising tendencies of the retrograde planet, the house it rules in the chart will inherit the same quality. Thus, if Mars is retrograde, then the house having the sign Aries on the cusp will be compromised for other houses ruled by the planets in oppositions to Mars.

For example: Retrograde Mars opposite Venus, Aries rising, Tarus on the second house cusp and Libra will be on the seventh house cusp. Here Martian energies give in to Venus, or sex compromised for love. In the same fashion, first house will sacrifice for the spouse. Consequently, first house will be given lesser priority over the second house. Thus, values overtake personality or individuality compromised and sacrificed towards building resources. If, in the above example, Venus was retrograde opposite regular Mars, then all the priorities, adaptabilities, compromises, and give-ins will be exactly opposite. There the first house will gain superiority over second and seventh house. This will be over and beyond what other things would be in the rest of the chart. Thus actual house locations of the retrograde planets may not be as important as the houses they rule in the natal chart for the deductive interpretation. Under intercepted situations, the same is true but through implicit or indirect ways. In that case, the house will have a surface ruler (sign on the cusp) and an indirect ruler (ruler of the sign intercepted in that house). By knowing both of these rulers and their direct or indirect motion, one would judge the house performance.

For example: Aries rising and Tarus intercepted in the first house. Mars is direct but Venus retrograde. Then outwardly the person will be as usual as Aries rising but due to Venus retrograde ruling the interception, his inner personality will exhibit compromises, adaptability, flexibility, and sudden inferiorities with indecisions. Here both rulers are important, but they manifest through different channels.

RETROGRADES AND INTERCEPTIONS

The intercepted signs and intercepted planets behave quite implicitly or indirectly contrary to their basic character. The interceptions become problem issues for the native to overcome in order to fully justify their total expressions. The visible lack of freedom to release the potent energies of the interceptions create complexities and under estimations within that chart. When a retrograde planet rules a sign that is intercepted in that chart, all the learning and relearning experiences, compromises, and adaptabilities, fluctuations, indecisions, uncertainties, and diffused qualities are operating on a level below the normal surface. The planetary qualities will be down played, implicitly expressed and often consumed within the native. Substantial inner growth and inner healing are noticed here at the cost of parasitical self-nourishment. The energies that are produced inside remain inside on a larger scale. This gives an impression of an inefficient human mechanism for the usage of that energy. The planet may be inhibited to export his qualities or not given a competitive chance to evaluate itself in the light of the intereacting environment. Self-sufficiencies are created within, or they are forced upon the native due to the phenomenon. As an example, Retrograde Mars with the sign Aries intercepted in the chart will be much more capable to suppress its energies, hostilities, temper, aggression, etc. He will have a difficult time in "field testing" his intensity, or he may not know his true strength. This is done at the expense of suppressed energies inside. He periodically doubts his capabilities. His power of will remains a myth to him. When desperately needed or forced to use his energies, he often overdoes his things and appears much stronger Martian. However, due to internal entrapment, it is equally possible that he may burn himself in the show of force and execution.

Similarity a retrograde planet in an intercepted sign will be inhibited, withhold or downplay its role due to circumstances, compared to his normal activities. The combinations of these two, when fully enclosing in nature are most difficult to handle in maintaining a justified balance of energies in the life of that person. Just for example, Retrograde Saturn in the intercepted Cancer or Capricorn sign. Here Saturn is intercepted in a sign and the sign it rules is also intercepted in that chart.

RETROGRADES IN GROUPS

The grouping of retrograde planets can be a study in itself. They do not even have to have interelating aspects to bind uniqueness together. The groupings can be done two at a time or three or more together. Such combinations run into several hundreds and are beyond the scope of this text. However, typical mention of some groupings can be studied here and the rest of it is left open to the logical imagination of the readership.

- **Subjective Domain:** Existence of retrogrades only in the subjective side of the chart (Houses 10 through 3) will indicate learning lessons through one's own need to control life. Inability to have a total faith in oneself.
- **Objective Domain:** Retrogrades occupying this section of the chart alone (Houses 4 through 9) will indicate mild confusions, uncertainties, and indecisions towards one's objectivity. Life remains in the hands of others but the native is not fully aware of the consequences.
- **Above the Horizon:** All the retrogrades above the horizon indicate strong need for public life with or without complicated challenges. He attracts others' attention irrespective of its quality. Needs to be out in the open, hustling for success. Drives hard to get to his goals in spite of repeated frustrations. Eventually compromises public status for domestic bliss.
- **Below the Horizon:** All the retrogrades below the horizon indicate a need for privacy and internal happiness. He tries hard to get the focus away from him to achieve something meaningful in life without arousing public attention. Prefers to be introverted without realizing why. Eventually, this life pattern is compromised to achieve things in the public eye. Introversion becomes a confinement from

which the native rescues himself.
- **Northeast or Intuitive Section:** Learning lessons from his own intuitive decisions. Irrationalism or reversals in his own gut feelings. Diffused intuition makes deductions uncertain. Following the wrong hunch possible. He tries hard to perfect his intuitive capabilities.
- **Northwest or feeling section:** Uncertainties in the feeling areas or not knowing when and how to apply them. Diffusion or foggy attitude towards recognizing one's own feelings. Complicated romances and chances taken with repeated errors as the native does not feel right about the situations. Misunderstands other's feelings towards him. Learns through feelings.
- **Southwest or Sensation Section:** Learns from sensations. Sensationalism is very important and challenge creating in life. Gets attracted by sensation but has to face the reality of pleasurism.
- **Southeast or Thinking Section:** Complicated thinking, decision making on a logical level but fails to follow through with them. Excessive thinking, complications in career and subsequent changes in life goals. Disruptions in friendships or friendships become mutually learning situations. A lot of action in life in the subjective but public domain.
- Personal planets such as Mercury, Venus, and Mars create learning experiences and repetitions from individual events, personality, attitudes, self expressions and interpersonal situations. You create your own problems in order to grow from their learning experience. Personal life becomes the proving grounds with variations, uncertainties, and readjustments. Need to reestablish your personal goals and individual values in relation to others seen here.
- Planets Jupiter and Saturn in retrograde combination create learnings through the surrounding environment, neighbors and nearby society. The people in the nearby vicinity, family structure, traditions, and relatives bring challenging situations to overcome in the native's life. Their hindrance and support are equally important in his life as the learning tools.
- Outer Planets, Uranus, Neptune, and Pluto in retrograde combination create learnings from the universal worldly situations. The society as a whole becomes crucial in modifying his personality, attitudes, and goals. Here the socioeconomic universality brings awareness to him. Either he changes through that enlightening experience or makes a great impression upon others utilizing those means. No one-to-one situations are greatly contributing to his growth but dealing with impersonalized learnings are of main essence here. Universal awareness, metaphysics, spirituality and mass Karma can be well associated with this native. He respects and abides by the outer forces and at times even rebels against them just to show his spunk.
- Retrograde combination involving both of the same character planets such as Mercury-Uranus, Venus-Neptune, and Mars-Pluto indicate distortions or inefficient usage of those functions. Here both Mercury and Uranus will create mental fluctuations, or uncommon thinking. It would indicate learning difficulties or ultra intellectual individual unable to use his mental energies.

- The rulers of the houses 1,4,5,9, and 10 are very favorable in life. Having several of them retrograde in the chart will indicate the uncertainty the native has in recognizing the good decisions. The efforts are exerted by shooting in the dark to achieve proper spiritual direction in life. Eventually, he finds his place in life, accepting the retrogradation as hindrance rather than a total failure in life.
- Retrogrades in Elements: When all the retrogrades are contained in one element, (3 or more), these elemental qualities will show different characters. Disintegrations, defractions, diffusions, and improper estimation of the appropriate qualities seen in that native. Thus, from fire elements, improper self assertiveness, energy imbalance, sudden withdrawls of physical staminas or "go-get" spirit takes a nap all of a sudden. Internal rebellion is created in these combinations for that element. This contamination of the element requires proper attention by the native and over compensation periodically to neutralize the influence.

RETROGRADE IN PROGRESSIONS

Since this book is mainly focused towards retrogrades in the natal chart, predictive methods are of least consideration in this text. The totality of the book should not be applied towards the progressed charts as it can be a much different state of existence. Even though the rules for static existence (natal chart) can be similar to dynamic behavior (progressions) in the life of that native, considerable differences have to be taken into account. In order to avoid lengthy pages on this topic, brief points to be considered are as follows:
- When a planet turns retrograde several days after birth, it will show an impact upon the life of that native in a manner described by the secondary progressions. The planetary qualities will begin to modify, change, and adjust appropriately at that age described by the corelation from the secondary progressions.
- Changes in the quality of that planet from direct to retrograde are significant from then on.
- Changes in the areas of life governed by the house(s) ruled by that planet will show substantial significance. For example: Mars going retrograde will affect the house ruled by Aries. Thus, an ascendant will undergo strong changes of personality, self power, individual energies, personal magnetism, etc. If Aries was on the fifth house cusp in the natal chart, the person will see changes in his dynamic creativity, sport orientations, risky chance takings, impulsive but sensation needs in romance, impatience towards children, active expressions of talents, etc.
- The changes begin to show appropriately within a matter of several months corresponding to the changes in direction of that planet described by the secondary progressions. Faster moving planets, such as Mercury will react much sooner, than the slower moving Pluto in the secondary progressions. For many outer planets, a stationary period exists around the time of retrogradation. In such cases, the effects of changes in direction take several years to manifest in the life of that native. An element of acceleration and deceleration plays crucial factor

in determining the timing of transition. The native is programmed under one condition and cannot be instantly deprogrammed just because planet changes direction. Memory clearing takes time and the effects are altered in a matter of a couple of years before and after the actual turning points occur.
* The house occupied by the progressed planet when it changes direction has the least significance. However, the natal house occupied by its natal position is very important along with the natal house rulerships.

RETROGRADES IN TRANSITS

A transiting planet has almost an invariable influence whether it is direct or retrograde in motion for most of the delineations. Minor variations and points of differences are created by virtue of its forming and separating directions. The qualities of the planet which is transiting will be very much the same under any situations. The timing factor and arousal reactions differ for direct and retrograde motion.
* Thus a first approach of the direct transiting planet will be a warning signal, awareness building and background establishment for that transit.
* When that planet retrogrades in transit and repeats the same aspect as before, internal adjustments, delayed reactions, and rearranged responses occur. This is quite an unexpected situation for the person and the planet which is being transited. The approach is unique, different, and far from anticipated. As a result, most of the internal reactions occur at this time frame. Any uncertainities prior to this are weighed again as a second chance. The decisions to resist, react, or remain neutral are made at this junction. There may or may not be any explicit action at this time, but internal functions take into account everything relating to the decision making.
* When the same transiting planet goes direct and repeats the same aspect, judgement situation is present. Now or never dilemmas are present here. Any leftover hesitancy will be overcome at this time and events or reactions precipitated. If nothing happens by now, it will not occur in that combination. All transits do not always produce significant effects anyway.

As a result of this all, the second stage, when a retrograde transit is in effect, most of the psychological warfare, reactions, decision making and crucial execution of energy unfolding occurs here.

For more discussions of variable event/formation under multiple transiting conditions of the planet due to retrogradation, refer to the book *Precise Progressed Charts by Koparkar.*

RETROGRADES AND REINCARNATION

The retrograde motion is often associated with the concept of reincaration by way of perfecting one's soul. This perfection or purification process ponders the person regarding the repetitious learning experiences. Due to retrograde motion, events occur first and the true awareness of their consequences comes later. In a way, this appears as a meant-to-be process. What we did not know becomes a reality of awareness that is considered as fate or destiny. For this reason, Lunar Nodes are highly associated with Karma and one's learning program in life because of their constant backward motion. In a similiar fashion, retrograde planets indicate what is meant-to-be in certain situations emphasizing the fate associated with it. In order to perfect one's soul, the repetition of the life forms and successive experiences are essential. This is achieved through the retrograde planets in that life. These planets provide the clues as to which learning experiences need to be redone or perfected. More retrogrades often indicate that the person has to work hard to achieve the same results as compared to someone with no retrogrades. Retrograde planets are not the degrading experiences but opportunities to get the important on the job training. In a way, having retrograde planets indicates the direction of life which needs to be properly looked at with serious interest. People with many retrograde planets may be fulfilling many repetitions in life to neutralize the balance of Karma on their accounts. People with no retrogrades have other things to learn and achieve, may be given retrogrades the next time around, if they fail to achieve their missions in this life time. You cannot perfect something unless you initiate it. An existence of mistake in itself indicates efforts and a scar of being there. Looking from this far sighted approached, retrogrades appear as a blessing no matter how hard their existance can be in the ongoing life struggle.

RETROGRADES IN MUNDANE ASTROLOGY

The retrograde motion of the planet plays significant roles in the everyday, mundane situation. Keeping in mind what is good for one individual may be compensated by another. Here the significant difference between the direct and retrograde motion of a planet is spread over a large selection of population with local peaks. This is not to say a retrograde Mercury will be causing total havoc or change in the communication system of the world. Chances are, more people are affected in this transition from direct to retrograde than those who are not. The people who are aware of this information seem to get more affected by this transition than the others under similar circumstances. The minor effects of the reversals in planetary motions are definitely present, but their true intensity is hard to judge and justify on simple conclusions of retrogradation alone. It would be a whole book in itself to evaluate the impact of retrogrades on mundane events and how they affect certain classes of individuals. The overall analysis of a retrograde

Mercury delaying the communication is reasonably correct, but it does not truly help anyone in particular. Knowing the mail system or any telephone company, these snags are present periodically, but certainly coincide during the three special Mercury retrogradations annually. In short, keeping in mind the transition of the planetary direction of motion may affect you or the system you participate in. However, it is not something one can totally rely upon. Individual natal charts are better guidelines than the overall mundane influences. Combining the natal character with a finishing touch by mundane influences will give a fairly good analysis for that individual.

Due to variations in perodicity of planets under retrograde conditions, it is hard to avoid doing certain things under certain retrograde planets. For example, when Saturn goes retrograde, it maintains its retrograde status for several months. It is difficult to say do not take up a new job under these conditions. The statement has some merit since Saturn rules the natural tenth house of profession and any major decisions of actions regarding that area should have the proper blessing of the direct motion of that planet. However, looking from a global viewpoint, thousands and even millions of people change jobs under retrograde Saturn. I admit, most of them will change jobs again soon, but that could happen whether Saturn was direct or retrograde when they last changed their jobs. From a more logical standpoint, if the native has Capricorn on the tenth house cusp or Saturn in that house or Saturn direct in the chart, he should avoid changing careers and professions under retrograde Saturn period. This is likely to give him better odds to fight the circumstances or take advantage of the good potential.

Under retrograde condition of any planet, avoid initiating new things related to that planet provided the same planet emphasizes that from the natal chart. For example: Under retrograde Mercury avoid contracts, paper, news releases, new plans for business, new learning or teaching, etc. in general. However, based on your natal chart, you can narrow down what to avoid under these situations. Thus, if you have Gemini on the second house, then avoid financial contract. Virgo on the seventh cusp, then avoid marriage under retrograde Mercury. If Mercury rules the fourth house, then do not sign lease or make an offer on the house purchase. Similarily, if Saturn rules the second house, then do not change jobs at that time as long as your motivation is not to add resources. Thus, areas ruled by a planet in the natal chart are likely to show least benefits and even frustrations in certain cases, if one tries to initiate them under the retrograde motion of that planet. Any other beginnings that are not controlled or influenced by that planet can be undertaken during the retrograde motion without any problems.

If you start anything under retrograde motion and finish it before the planet goes direct, you are seldom affected in the area ruled by that planet. It is the barrier of transition from retrograde to direct motion that obstructs and blocks the path of success of that event.

The retrograde motion in mundane astrology is a vast area and individual applications should be tailored for that person alone based upon his original conditions of existence.

RETROGRADE MERCURY

Internalizing and externalizing of information can be associated with some impedences in this case. As a result, the native will comprehend and express as usual, but he would have difficulty confirming what he learned. Instant recall can meet internal resistance and hesitancy. The process of the information flow through this native can be complex. He can be as smart as others, but he may not be able to show it all the time. Learning through normal logic, as well as reverse logic is seen here. This can confuse the brain periodically. Deductive reasoning and utilizing methods of elimination can be prominant in this case. He fluctuates from either extremes of intelligence to a noncomprehendable individual. Unique way of externalizing gives him added advantage to mix with other people. Normal senses work overtime, but not necessarily on a standard routing. He needs time to digest his information, learnings, and categorize it. He will talk smart, when he does not know the subject. On the other hand, he can play dumb when he is sure of his knowledge and information. Learning through feedback from others is extremely natural for him. Thus, he would rather interchange his ideas, participate with cooperative learning -teaching than be a straight forward communicator. He respects others intelligence, but he may not be sure of himself. Self examination, reconfirmation, inner evaluation and periodic information retrival are very important to him. Mental confusions, excessive thinking or his ideas become too big for him. Repeated clarifications are expected by him and his curiosity may appear pesty or blunt to others. Excellent service orientation noticed here and on the job performance is associated with constant learning. This learning to keep up with the state of the art is important no matter what the art can be. Unusual relationship with brothers and sisters seen. At one point, they are very close to the native and then all of a sudden totally separate due to circumstances. Some mental distress, agony, or confusing issues occur from the mother's side of the family. Substantial difference is noticed in his early school performance and later education. Often the native may not use his learnings or formal education towards his true professional achievements. In social function, he can be an exciting individual to observe as he can switch topics and sides of conversations right in the middle. Mental stimulations are important to him on the job, but at home he may want to detach from the strainy brain interactions. A childish or youngish expression and behavior often seen here as the native can maintain better youthfulness in life than others. However, outwardly getting grey hair early in life compensates towards his maturity. Diversification, learning the same thing again, or lack of coordination towards learning are noticed. This repeated process may not be due to thoroughness but rather an absentminded tendency. Nervous system, reflexes, speech patterns, brain wave functions, witty combat, devil's advocate, complex thinking in terms of strategies, mild mental distortions, etc. can be possible and need attention periodically. Good logic is seen here but the native may lack self confidence or self trust in his own ideas and their execution.

RETROGRADE MERCURY THROUGH THE HOUSES

Retrograde Mercury Through The First House. Self-conscious, mentally indecisive, delays in decisions, uncertain communications. Repeated learning, insecure of his own ideas. Self-worth fluctuates, ideas in transition, mature when young, but childish in older years, easily persuaded. Learns quickly but forgets easily. Mental drain or depressions caused by own faults. Sincerely tricky, promises more than he can deliver.

Retrograde Mercury Through The Second House. Good money making ideas without thorough practicality. Speech as an asset or liability, talks a lot about money, values big business, security in expression, mental approach to life values, abrupt financial reversals, losses through brothers/sisters, impulsive to ideas in application but delays in reactions. Information converted to assets but lack of concentration becomes liability.

Retrograde Mercury Through The Third House. Talkative, communicative but changes his arguments easily. May not be reliable for his promises. Always in need for better understanding, eager to learn, jack of all trades, but may not master anything. Concepts more important than details. Theorizes everything, swifty, impatient and nervous. Mental reiterations, revolving ideas and reevaluates strategy constantly. Argues with brothers/sisters, enjoys good arguments and discussions. Imbalance in learning and understanding. Extremistic as a student.

Retrograde Mercury Through The Fourth House. Active at home, good ideas towards life security. A sense of purpose cultivated inside, introvert, family oriented or depends upon the family. Insecure in expressions, works his ideas through others. Resents idealogy of mother but follows her pattern very well. Complexes through real-estate contracts, logic and emotions fight within him, withdraws under pressure. Idea germination blooms in future. Illogical family tradition, needs to know family history.

Retrograde Mercury Through The Fifth House. Mental creativity, self-conscious in romance, likes children only when young. Ideas vacillate regarding pleasurism. Too much or too little expressions in interpersonal matters. Speculative ideas present but gains not predictable. Childish attitude, lack of concentration in early education. Mother's worth in doubt, indulges in mental fantasies. Popular with friends, adapts creativity easily, gambles with mental resources.

Retrograde Mercury Through The Sixth House. Nervous on the job, service oriented, ideas in motion, undertakes a lot of responsibility at work, stomach/digestive difficulties, nervous stress created. Work pressure affects health, improper diet, mental guidance not properly listened on the job. Minor distorted family relations from mother's side. Takes things for granted regarding on-the-job training, constantly thinking about spouse and other's opinions. Ideas and efforts do not blend, inner insecurities projected through work. Nervous breakdown potential.

Retrograde Mercury Through The Seventh House. Too much or too little communicative in marriage, goes back on promises, distorted objectivity, adapts others' outlooks but resents it later, mental/intellectual gap needed in partnership, partnership comprehended well on a mental level but reality differs, childish plays in marriage, idea of marriage stimulates him more than marriage itself. Attracts others through mental magnetism, judges people by their mentality rather than physical exterior, shrewd, diplomatic, tactful, mediator, presents himself well to others.

Retrograde Mercury Through The Eighth House. Mental preoccupation with sex and morbid thoughts, needs to know, penetrates under the surface, interest in the occult, strategy justified more than the end results, good ideas regarding finances, credit, and corporate resources. Interests in occult, deaths, reincarnations, and life after death, psychological encounters, perceptions, practicality, ponderance preempt his mind to learn new innovation, jealous, intense and sharp thinker, conflicts with combined values in marriage, mismatched in sexual communication.

Retrograde Mercury Through The Ninth House. Exaggerates, over estimates and logicizes philosophies, takes the middle road as far as world events, difficulties in higher education or may not be able to use higher education for practical usage. Illogical philosophies create his unique beliefs, moving away from brothers/sisters, marketing, sales, publications, institutional knowledge, or legal contracts, ideas differ with the standardized institutions, wisdom fights the common sense, abrupt departures, linguistic.

Retrograde Mercury Through The Tenth House. Changes career in the middle of life, more than one defined career goals, ideas important to follow through than the actual support of others, differences with father, verbal arguments with authority. Under pressure, he can be nervous, expressive and talkative, seriousness and cautiousness displayed. Impotency due to career anxiety, good follower as long as ideas blend well. Recognition through his ideas and expressions.

Retrograde Mercury Through The Eleventh House. Friendships fluctuate, enjoys verbal arguments and differences. Mental reactions appreciated by friends. Change in profession in middle third of life. Abrupt changes in group association. Mentality differs with others on simple tactical issues. Problems with offspring, learning lessons through friendships, mental difference needed with friends, can be antisocial, introversion strikes him unexpectedly. Unique ideas, rebellious but high strong social view points, inventiveness but he outsmarts himself.

Retrograde Mercury Through The Twelfth House. Hidden stress and anxiety, unusual ideas regarding spirituality, reincarnation, perceptions, impressions and intuitiveness but cannot apply them to himself, vast subconscious but non-communicative, digests his learnings and preserves them, foggy perspectives of life. Mental intoxications, mental withdrawals and spiritual communications, mediumistic, learns through symbology and osmosis, fantasizes a lot, good idea generation, but slow externalization. Success late in life, senile tendencies in later years, usually long life.

RETROGRADE MERCURY RULING THE HOUSES

Retrograde Mercury Ruling the First House. Self doubt may be present in the native as he evaluates both sides of the situation. Uncertainties as to the long term impact of his decision making are seen. He can change his mind very easily as he gets to know more information regarding the situation. Speech and power of expression fluctuates in this case as he undergoes variations in his self-confidence. He wants to learn things his own way, but others can influence his choice easily. Gullibility, trustworthy nature, and diffused perceptions may be noticed in him. Ability to contradict himself get him in and out of trouble unexpectedly. Work attitudes may not be consistent here as the native can be moody and casual about it. The distorted or defracted sense of services may not win him any awards on the job but coworkers like him. Nervous anxiety, often associated with abrupt depressions, contributes to lower his efficiency of production. Personality differences with brothers and sisters may bring verbal battles or communication blackouts. Sudden urge to travel may be created within, but he compromises for a short coffee break. He has to learn a lot about himself as he unfolds in life. Reversals in introversions to extroversion or vice versa are expected here as he grows older. Childish, immature or innocent expression often gets him out of trouble in early life. Plans and counter plans are important as he enjoys mental stimulation and instigation.

Retrograde Mercury Ruling the Second House. Good money making ideas are produced within him constantly. However, he may not have the courage of his convictions to put then toward practical use. All talk but no action makes him unproductive in the financial areas. His advice and consultation may be taken by many but he doubts his own capabilities. His own finances he can manage well once he believes in the goals. Accounting, statistics, detail management, financial counselling, brokerage exchanges, credit, banking, etc. can be significant here. Mental thought is crucial for him. For that reason, he should be learning, updating his knowledge and get on-the-job exposure periodically. Stubborn attitudes or self-conscious nature may be seen that do not deviate from his basic stand in life. Idealism, fantasies, and carefree attitudes towards combined resources seen here. Make-believe sensations created by him or he enjoys individualized pleasure fairly strong. Ability to help others in need is excellent, giving him supporting hand from others when he needs it. Mental craftiness can be seen, but he simply enjoys the value of the game plan more than anything else. With brothers and sisters, financial issues arise bringing complications. Thus, he has a lot to learn regarding how to collect and enjoy it simultaneously.

Retrograde Mercury Ruling the Third House. Talkative and communicative nature of this individual is well appreciated by others in a unique way. Extremes in expressions noticed here along with great adaptability to what others want to hear. Verbal retreat is shown by the native rather than relatiation. He can be a loud mouth critic as easily as he can be a gullible sufferer. His strategies may be shallow as they are tailored towards short run impact. On a long range planning schedule, he has to evaluate and modify his decisions frequently. Love of travel may be compromised for mental fantasies. His mind can be far reaching and penetrating when he has deep gut feelings. The relationships with brothers and sisters are fluctuating. Thus, he may be much closer to them all of a sudden, and then he detaches from them. He has a good mind, but it may not portray well in terms of school grades. Indecisive logic and reversals in the decision making lower his personality strength. Actually, his thinking and ideas are slightly out of phase with the existing times. Community support dwindles towards him as the native goes around in the circle with his great ideas without productive end results. He can be speechless when he is thinking, or it is hard for him to coordinate expressions and production of thoughts at the same time. Unusual but inconsistent handwriting may be seen here. Contractual agreements often need revisions of the text, otherwise they backfire upon the native.

Retrograde Mercury Ruling the Fourth House. The native is slightly uncertain of his mental stability due to early upbringing. His ideas, thinking and communication can be highly influenced by his mother or the inactive parent. A sense of tradition controls his thoughts and externalization. However, as he grows older, he unwinds completely and forms his own mental channels. The security and roots of life are verbalized and mentally visualized rather than emotionally felt. Very logical and intellectual approach to events at home noticed as the native feels more comfortable to that type of relating than anything else. Intellectually stimulating early life seen, but communicative stresses with mother are possible. Later in life, he rebels away from his family roots and traditions. Home front is much more flexible compared to career demands on this native. Real estate, property, lands, and material benefits are often shared with brothers and sisters on unequal basis. Some family ties in terms of old spirits and mystical communication with them can be likely. He acts quite innocent and childish at home. As a result, he blends well with children on a sympathetic basis. Learning at home rather than at school can be important to him as the homey atmosphere stimulates his intellectual circuits. Learning lessons from home matters seen here. As a result he may have to readjust to various home surrroundings and possible relocations. Success away from home or away from the family seen eventually in the life of this native.

Retrograde Mercury Ruling the Fifth House. Communication problems or improper communication can be seen in love/romance. Romantic intensity may not be verbalized or easily comprehended by the native. Emotions and their understanding can be out of phase for this person making him appear less responsive in the interaction. He takes mental approach when the other person expects emotional reaction and vice versa. This causes certain problems in the relationship on the surface but the inside of the interaction can be good and secure. Lower education will not show as good a promise as the native could in the higher learning. This occurs due to lack of concentration in early ages towards structured education. Mental creativity can be excellent and expressive with great ideas. However, the native may not have the persistence to follow through his creative dreams. He needs an extra person or partner to get them off the ground towards fulfillment. Social interactions are significant to him, but strictly on a mental stimulating level. Good communication with children is noticed here as the native can truly experience their side and understand it. However, later in life sudden reversals are possible which cause communicative blockouts with children. Good mental strategies and ideas are available to him but he may not be sure of them to win consistently through speculative means. Periodic verbal combat shown by him to rescue his family more than himself from outside situation.

Retrograde Mercury Ruling the Sixth House. Changes in work often occur as his attitudes towards the services he provides fluctuate. Sudden reversals in the opinions on the job make him isolated from the coworkers. In a way, it is hard for him to know who his friends are and who expresses dissatisfactions towards him on the job. As a result, he does his duty and then detaches from the scene. Although the job makes him nervous, he handles the situation in a cool manner, but he takes his problems home. This can be difficult to his family as they do not want to aggrevate him any more than he already is. They just have to accept him and his job related anxiety or pressure as long as they can. Nervous disorder, poor diet, ill decisions, improper financial planning for children, and easy habit formation are seen here. Complex issues regarding the cousins on the mother's side of the family can be noticed here. Father often does not recieve as much recognition or publicity as expected. This hurts the native psychologically and he tries to overcompensate that by achieving something equal or better than his father to please him. Fluctuating appetite, irregularities in the food intake and nervousness contribute to a difficult stomach-intestinal system. In work related areas, he switches his opinions in the groups or unions but benefits from it eventually. Indirect communication in marriage or partnership seen here as third party meadiator may be present or needed.

Retrograde Mercury Ruling the Seventh House. Business partnerships require careful attention here as misunderstandings and miscommunications grow out of proportion. Contractual agreements, legal representations and communicative commitments undergo periodic changes forcing the partnership into troubled waters. The native has fluctuating objectivity and his stands on key issues change abruptly. In marriage, he tries to justify everything on a mental level, forcing communication of feelings from the spouse. Subsequently, partnership displays rebellion and communication blackouts. He may be in love with the idea of marriage rather than loving the marriage itself. He can be blunt towards open enemies and the threats are mostly verbal in format. His public opinion changes frequently as he can be dualistic towards others. Learning through others can be important to him. Thus, his information comes from reflection through others than his own efforts to learn on his own. This reflection of ideas works in another way to reinforce what mental capabilities have already comprehended. Split tongue may be seen in his communication, but that can be his asset in terms of politics, representations, law, mediations, and salesmanship. Information and general knowledge are more important to him than actual depths and details. Some mental difficulties or minor abnormalities are possible to the grandparent, and they may even be inherited through that channel.

Retrograde Mercury Ruling the Eighth House. Mismatched sexual communication or imbalanced signal exchange is noticed here. What the native wants and how he asks for it are in disharmony regarding his physical drive and sexual sensation. It is possible he intellectualizes his inner base needs and satisfies the quench on a mental level. Knowledge, information, and mental stimulation are closely associated with his animalistic passion. However, he has difficulty evaluating the true fulfillments and their origin. The mild variations of sexuality could be the root foundation in his abberations towards these base fulfillments. Sexuality defraction may not be on a practical mundane basis, but rather on a mental level. His attitudes towards combined resources can be logical and straight forward without emotional hindrance. Spouse may not contribute financially as much as the native expects. As a result, combined contributions are given higher priority in judging, the true relationship than anything else. He may talk a lot about credit, corporations, general finances, economy, insurance matters, and other business liabilities/assets; but his actual contributions and gains through this all may not be significant. He enjoys mental stimulations through them much more than actual involvement. Inheritance may be hindered through brothers/sisters or legal complications of the actual text cause frustrations to him in this case. Sudden mental withdrawals or communication blackouts are likely here.

Retrograde Mercury Ruling the Ninth House. The native switches his beliefs easily or finds most philosophies in proper logic. As a result, he can be convinced of different faiths by different people. Fluctuating standards of life give him excellent sense of experimentation. Mild insecurities may be seen in externalizing his philosophies towards others. He is not sure of the advantage of the higher education. As a result, he may neglect those pursuits without serious thoughts. Language, linguistic ability, and innovative communication with people of different culture and background can be seen here. He understands things as long as there are some philosophical concepts associated with them. This mystical/philosophical grasp for practical learning helps him in early life. Concepts become key elements than the total information. He exaggerates and talks a lot. Over estimation of his mental capabilities are likely in this case, but he would never think he is doing that. Reversals in legalities or litigations are possible, but his own self defense becomes his worst enemy. When applicable, second marriage issue provides a lot of communicative stresses or lack of mutual understanding. Thus, simple physical or emotional attraction might be present in it. Brother-in-laws and sister-in-laws play crucial role in making and breaking the marriage. Somehow, their hindrance is eventually felt. Unpredictable publicity may be received by him or he gets involved with volatile public issues without realizing them fully.

Retrograde Mercury Ruling the Tenth House. He often feels he is in the wrong profession or his expressions can be out of phase with respect to actual satisfactions. Thus, he would complain when happy on the job and keep quiet when miserable and dissatisfied. Improper communication or lack of it with father is noticed in early life. He had difficulty understanding the family discipline, tradition, or methodology. Somehow it did not register in his mind what their expectations can be regarding him. A slight distorted sense of respect or misunderstood authority complex seen here. The native competes with his father or tries to overdo his intellectual achievements. However, he seldom gets proper recognition for trying hard. Mother figure may not be significant in his life or she plays a shadow character in it. In his professional achievements, he tries to go after the goals in an indirect way. Thus, he does not get things as he did not ask for them. Under pressure, he is very talkative, expressive but indecisive. All the emergency plans freeze upon him under that pressure, making him nervous. He reacts abruptly and spontaneously. Communicative, intellectual or mental exposure can be significant on the job and he has to deal with people with or without his choice. Social recognition, fringe benefits, or publicity from the job may not be as much as he truly deserves.

Retrograde Mercury Ruling the Eleventh House. Disagreements with friends or basic differences of ideas are noticed in this case. The native changes his hopes and goals of life all of a sudden. As a result, what he hopes for in early teenage period regarding his future differs considerably when he gets there. Group associations do not remain consistent in his life as he hops around changing his participation. Intellectual and mental stimulation can be expected by him but his view points are not very compatible with them. His ideas and idealogy go in different directions as far as his participation with friendly interaction is concerned. His perspectives may be different, but he is happy by his own achievements. Love recieved can be uncertain to him as he never knows who his real friends are in any group activity. Social involvement may be done out of curiousity rather than actual needs and enjoyment. Idea exchanges with others give him the short end of the stick. In the long run he benefits from his old ideas which have been cultivated by someone else. Good impressionability is noticed here, but he can be withdrawn and aloof when he wants to. Step-children create some hassel in his life when applicable. He feels like a child all over again when he reaches his middle age. Getting involved with father's business or his business aptitude might be directly inherited by the native in this case.

Retrograde Mercury Ruling the Twelfth House. Previous life of this individual was spent in excessive mentally stimulating situations. Sharp mind is noticed here that he can recall from the past only when he needs it. Under normal situations he can be quiet, introverted, and introspective. He relies greatly on the past and how it would influence his future. Projecting the past to a successful future can be very important to him. However, he is not sure of the logic behind it, as to why it should be the case. Hidden matters or hidden phobias are analyzed by him rather than emotional chaos. Thus, his approach to resolving other's cloggged subsconscious will be very detail oriented and systematic. On his own, his logic fails him and he has to use instinctive means to get him out of his own fog. Fantasies remain his logical way out of many confining situations. He would rather underestimate himself and be pleased with pleasant surprise than be disappointed due to optimism later on. Mental sensations get to him or fantasized turn-ons are important for his moral boost. He may talk in his sleep, but he will not realize he does so. Psychic communication and acute gut feelings come true for him frequently. Behind the scene communication helps him get to his goals in life in later years. He works best under isolative environment.

RETROGRADE MERCURY OPPOSITE MOON

Sympathetic, apathetic, and self-sacrificial nature seen. Personal sensitivity gathers others problems very easily. Thus, the native may react to others situations very suddenly and at times irrationally. Getting nervous from other people or overly projecting self-phobias is seen in this case. Stability, security, and life foundations are given high priority in life as compared to mental growth or work areas. As a result, the native may sacrifice work for the sake of better family and home situations. Respect for mother is superbly seen, and the native learns very well through her blessings and efforts. Logic and emotions contradict within the native but the emotions often have the last minute priority. Thus, decisions are on feeling level rather than on any logic. Imagination overtakes any conformed strategy. Thus, the person will enjoy doing things free-floatingly rather than go by the book. Mental and intellectual insecurities are compensated for by vivid imaginations. The native takes pride in creative indulgence and fantasized deep withdrawal. This inward search helps him in self-understanding so that he can relate to others on a better level when needed. A lack of proper objectivity might be noticed as he can be very uncertain regarding his opinions and their impact upon others. Here he is more worried about hurting them than helping with his objectivity. Dealing with people, services, counselling, and emotional reciprocity can be important in this case. In a man's case, he is often attracted to a woman who may not be very intellectual, but quite sensitive. He likes her indecisive nature or his mental superiority over her. At times, that is exactly what he gets without looking for it. In a woman's case, this aspect provides fluctuating intelligence. Thus, she can be very smart over certain issues but then very poor in her choice of decisions. Her intellectuality fluctuates considerably over a period of time as well. Mental stability is very important for the native, even though others think quite differently on that topic. Early senile tendencies occur as the native grows older. Fantasies and vivid imagination provide excellent escape tools for the native all through life and especially in later years. Learning through reverse psychology can be most efficient to this native.

RETROGRADE MERCURY OPPOSITE MARS

Sharp and active mind noticed but impulsiveness often spoils his good plans. His inner indecision and reiteration drives his patience wild. Thus, he spontaneously acts without full sense of consequences. In spite of great inner thinking and strategies his actions proclaim the superiority. The bite can be worse than the bark in this case. Tact and diplomacy might be missing here as the native wants quick action. Sensation and real actions provide more scope to this person than just mentally worked-out plans. Self-confidence, superiority complex and self-assertiveness are seen here without the strong backing of the thorough planning from within. As a result, the native initiates many projects but may not finish most of them. Due to his rash and impatient personality on the job, he can be isolated or left alone. Thus, it is best he performs alone or in small groups. He needs to out-do any other family member no matter what the cost and consequences can be to him. Verbally combative and at times argumentative nature seen. Here the person presumes the coordination of his thinking and actions. However, his actions are much faster and thinking takes time to unfold. This discrepancy can be the root cause of many of his failures. He has to learn to use his mental approach and consequently provide patience to the deployment of his energies. Once this coordination is achieved, the native can do wonders. Physical sports, daredevil activities, calculated risks, combative involvement can be significant here. Good mathematical ability or sense of statistics can be present to help the native evaluate situations in life. Clumsiness, accident prone tendencies, or minor lack of energy coordination seen. Headaches, head injury, or migrains require attention in this case. In early education, sports and outdoor activities attract him a lot. As a result, he neglects basic learnings and begins to resent formal education. When allowed to liberate himself, he can be antiestablishment without sufficient reasoning. He will grow out of that as the time goes on. Mischievous, naughty, and rebellious tendencies seen in early childhood. Later in life they turn into pickiness, teasing, and even sarcasm. The native will have substantial power play, verbal battles, and imbalanced mutual communication with spouse. Unusual objectivity is noticed in this case by way of explosive reaction or total unpredictable withdrawal.

RETROGRADE MERCURY OPPOSITE JUPITER

Optimism takes over calculated risks making the native hopeful of his efforts. Thus, he may put his efforts in planning and just sit back for the resulting outcome. Exaggeration and over estimation requires control in this case. Philosophies and beliefs are given considerable priority over the mundane logic. Goals are justified through complex means. Services and efforts are repeated just to be perfect in the achievement. Political connections, interests, or involvements can be noticed here. The native has a strong faith which drives him to achieve things. Idealism gains superiority over details causing intermittent frustrations and failures. He requires a lot of efforts to coordinate his strategies. Goals are very attractive to him, but he can lose his perspectives in their achievements. Business, banking, teaching, learning institutions, marketing, sales, and presentations, etc. can be important exposures in his career areas. His efforts and services eventually bring him recognition and exposure. Higher mind can be a lot more powerful than simple lower mental details for him. Leadership ability can be worth noticing here. Somehow others have to follow him simply by faith. It is not easy for him to establish a track record of success before he gets to lead somebody or something. After strong internal conflicts within himself, the native turns to religion for answers. His respect for the heavenly supremacy grows as time goes on. In early school age period, he may not do so well as he would later in college. The conflict of logic and philosophy occurs within him, but he simply forces the logic to adapt the situation at the end. This sacrifice of the reasoning power makes him dualistic in his attitudes. Relatives away from home can be significant compared to just nearby family. Thus, his success away from home is quite likely. Some litigations involving brothers/sisters are possible and the native often wins at the end. A sense of universal justice hounds him from within making him fight for social, educational and philosophical issues of the mundane type. He is willing to sacrifice his work and services for betterment of his soul and spirituality. This is done by sticking to his pride and beliefs all the way.

RETROGRADE MERCURY OPPOSITE SATURN

A cloud of seriousness surrounds the native. Thinking may not be sharp and acute but quite practical. The native may appear like a wet blanket, slow in decision making and passive in thinking. Controlled optimism, along with lack of self-confidence can be visible here. The native needs time to reevaluate his plans and strategies in the framework of constantly changing practicality. Thus, his duality or uncertainty in precise decision making is seen. Mind and mentality has to abide by the cold practicality. Thus, his rationalism is often successful in the long run. He respects authority, superiority, and higher-ups while utilizing his brains. Work is often sacrificed and compromised for the sake of professionalism. Thus, title can be of utmost significance to him compared to the actual efforts that are put in it. His thinking can be well influenced by his blind ambition. As a result, he does not need much praise to get his ego boosted. Family tradition is quite important as his logic is closely related and highly influenced by it. Skepticism, blindly taking things for granted and periodic supersitions are visible here. Delays, problems, and hindrances in lower education seen as the native suddenly withdraws from others. This affects his thinking capabilities and decision making. He has to learn and relearn the same thing more than once. Patience is needed in his pursuit of knowledge. Strong discipline needs to be established before he begins to retain what he is learning. Communications and expressions undergo drastic reversals. Thus, he may abruptly freeze as if he has a mental block. Actually in that case, he is reevaluating what he is saying or comprehending. Business aptitude can be good especially in the areas relating to family enterprises. Due to his unusual relating ability with others, relationship with people of the opposite sex can be detached, slow, and periodically missing. Late marriage or convenient arrangements are often seen. Self-satisfied nature of this native does not demand outside complementation. Thus, he can be happy in his own way without taking an additional burden of an extra person in his life. A sense of existing responsibility is very thoroughly embedded in him which he will not unload upon anyone else. Mental block or nervous freeze requires periodic attention by way of externalizing the inner build up from time to time.

RETROGRADE MERCRY OPPOSITE URANUS

Nervous distress and distorted reflexes seen here but the native may do a good job of hiding them. Constant thinking and continuous mental process seen. However, the native may not be so sure as to what he is thinking about. He may find himself in vicious circles as to the logic of decision making. He can be logical but he wants a unique outcome or unusual solution to every situation. Not being happy by common and average solutions takes him all over in the mental emptiness. Uncommonness or uniqueness becomes the goal of life. Exceptional mental capabilities can be possible if he can curb his far-outness. Others think of him as innovative, eccentric, and nutty at times. Computer like brain may be seen in many of these cases. Friendships are important and a lot of learning and communicative interactions occur through it. They can be responsible for the native's uniqueness. Here the person wants to out-shine his friends or catch up to their level of intelligence. In doing so, he has to work hard to acquire that status. Friendships gain superiority or priority over brothers and sisters. Thus, he may be more comfortable with them rather than in the family. Goals are favored compared to actual work that goes on to attain them. Thus, the end justifies the means to the native. Group associations will be important and the person would involve in various mental and work related associations. The native may have the peculiarity to make his friends nervous or he gets on their nerves. It occurs unconsciously or he tries very hard to be their friend and acquire confidence. This overdoing or self-sacrifice may pay off in terms of learning experiences from it after the friendship is over. Mental games or logical strategies can be significant. The challenges are often accepted and he indulges in putting his brain to work. Speech and communicative distortions are possible as the nervous build-up can explode within him. Unpredictable attitude is visible outwardly along with unique, independent nature. Being a black sheep of the family can be noticed. Good mathematical ability, numbers and statistics, geometric perspectives, or unusual innovate ideas in the making, are seen. Habit forming nature can be significant as it provides continuous belief to his nervous system. It is very hard for him to sit still and be calm. A lack of concentration is possible as nervous sensation surges constantly.

RETROGRADE MERCURY OPPOSITE NEPTUNE

Indecisions due to added inner confusion are noticed here. Logic and instincts clash with a last minute priority given to the instincts. The gut feelings, psychic perceptions or the sixth sense somehow controls the thinking function within the native. Some divine force guides the native in the decision making. In the long-run, he knows why he made that decision, but at the time he cannot truly justify his logic. Self sacrifice or compromised services to some idealistic goals seen. Escape, fantasies, and runaway attitudes are strong and the native uses them frequently on a mental level. Addictive tendencies or habit formation can be easy as the will power is weak in the native. Communication often requires reinforcement or he has to justify more than once what he truly means in his externalization. Learning difficulties can be seen as the environment may not be harmonious to his sixth sense. The osmosis from the surroundings, which helps him gather information and deductions, requires proper conditions. In a normal social structure, he may not get those conditions affecting his learning capabilities. Learning and relearning experiences from mentality, mannerism and attitudes seen. Work becomes confining, but he performs best under isolative conditions. Fantasies and vivid dreams provide him good creative ideologies to pursue in life. Work and surrounding family situations often hinder in his way to achieve spiritual escapism. Thus, in life, he has to work hard, provide services and keep his surrounding family content. When he gets bored with the worldly hide and seek, he simply withdraws within, hiding from the totality. Sudden attack of introversion, withdrawals and uncommunicativeness is possible. Nervous disorder, affected reflexes, and delayed reactions likely. Excellent acting and immitation capabilities seen here but more on a verbal level. Impressions, mime, method acting, silent expressions, etc. are quite possible and of interest to the native. Changes in diet often occur in life and fluctuations in work-service areas will almost coincide with it. Nursing, medicine and hospital connections can be significant one way or another. Considerable improved learning and mental alertness seen in the middle third of life. A sense of speech and hearing can be other than normal, either way.

RETROGRADE MERCURY OPPOSITE PLUTO

A lot of self doubts or insecurity regarding one's own thinking pattern noticed. Others' ideas may be more appealing than what the native comes up with. Considerable energies wasted within to judge the relative merit of subjective and objective ideas. The person can be sarcastic towards others or his reactions to others can be spunky. There are some transactional difficulties or communicative losses to and from others to him. Thus, he may misunderstand or misrepresent periodically the flow of the information with others. Mentality is self evaluative and self conscious. Gun-shy attitude or phobias to see hidden strategies around him. Thus, he may react to others before even they do anything to him. This mental hyperness affects his nerves and health at times. Habit forming is easy in this case. Dig deep attitude associated with need to know much more than what is on the surface drives him to constant penetration. He may even get on to others nerves or under their skin, without him knowing. He often plays smart when he does not know anything. On the other hand, he can be dumb, when he has the answers in his hands. Plans, strategies, and secrecies are important and significant with or without reasons. Learning difficulties may be noticed in early life as his attention is diverted to other things frequently. He learns through challenges or schemes provide him excellent background to gather information. Good money making ideas or ability to come up with nice schemes to boost the values and resources seen here. Hidden complex or inferiority created by brothers/sisters in his life. In order to overcome that impedence, he goes out of his way to prove to himself that he is as good or better than them. Slow but steady learning process seen here and the native underestimates his capability. Benefit of the doubt is given to others rather than to himself. Solving puzzles, games, or mystical coding and decoding seen here. Interest in the occult and metaphysics or even hypnosis likely. Mystery, science fiction, or para normal phenomenon can interest the native quickly. This person has the capabilities to suddenly withdraw and show introversion periodically. Very unusual approach and mentality toward sexuality seen here. Certain inner indecisions or inhibitions need to be overcome before the native gets into normality in that area.

RETROGRADE MERCURY OPPOSITE RETROGRADE MARS

Complex mentality, hostile verbal tendencies, and temperamental nature are seen here. Sharp and acute mind is possible, but the native has a tendency to misuse his brains. Hyperthinking or very slow logic can be likely. The basic inner dilemma as to the superiority of the brain or the brawn is seen here. Actions overtake strategy or thinking slows down actual zest. Basic plans and actions do not coordinate well or hinder in each others way creating chaos in actual dealing with the situation. The native becomes much too powerful or too brainy for himself. His strategies fall back upon him due to imbalance of the energies in action. Interactions with brother/sisters are very important but radically fluctuating. Accident prone tendencies, irrational acts, and minor clumsiness in motion seen. Here the impatience can be the culprit in his life. His logic justifies his actions. Then suddenly he takes more actions to jutify his logic. The process continues, and it is hard to control. In the work/service areas, he has difficulty getting along with others and vice versa. As a result changes in jobs or friendships on the job are seen frequently. Nervous rebellions, short temperament and verbal battles require calming down for the native. Good mathematical ability or at least dealing with numbers and logic are very important. Alertness, lack of sleep, insomnia, nervous disorder, strain in the brain, computer logic, cold decision making, blunt externalization, etc., can be seen. Under adverse conditions, accidents to the head, nervous system, or limbs are possible. A sense of hearing and speech pattern may undergo unusuality. Use of sign languages, lip-reading, or general coding and decoding can be very prominent. Sudden loss of memory, mental block or hysteria possible. When used in balance, this aspect can achieve excellent results. Quite complex mentality towards sex or unusual sexual ideas noticed. In a woman's case, sexual pleasurism has to be interpreted on a verbal sense. Mind is highly or closely related to the libido. Thus, sexuality gets truly controlled by the communication. In any case, verbalizing the actions are important for the inner fulfillments. Knowledge, understanding, and informational excess or total lack of it seen regarding sexuality. Incest potential on a real or fantasizing basis possible in this case.

RETROGRADE MERCURY OPPOSITE RETROGRADE JUPITER

Mental confusion, stresses, and inner indecisions are noticed here. Constant battle between logic and philosophies occurs within him. Goals and means modify each other frequently letting him run around in circles without explicit achievements in life. Strain in the brain gathers without conclusive efforts towards any purpose. Inconsistency in communication, expression, and externalization possible as nervous disharmony is present in this case. Conscious mind obstructs and interferes with the subconscious. Then an exact reverse phenomenon takes place. Multiple personality can arise out of this inner turbulence. When used with care and practicality, this native can perform like multiple identities in various directions. An ability to simultaneously maintain diverse focus upon key goals is possible. This exceptional talent is like walking on a thin ice, but the native can manage it superbly. Ideals have to clear the basic human logic. Thus, his personality fights his purposes from time to time. It is best, he goes for others purposes and goals in life as he can be objective about them. Life concepts, standards, morality, and ethics are preserved periodically and then suddenly sacrificed for human logic. The uncertainties may produce nervous breakdown potential. The dynamic thinking is visible and well projected upon others. Phobias of other people are suddenly internalized through osmosis by this native. He can submerge himself in various intricate interactions and maintain several communicative links separately at times. He works under most complex stimulations. It is hard to tell what drives him at times whether logic or just his faith. Superstitious tendencies under the cover of scientific background can be prominant here. Mentality varies from several years younger than him to considerably older for his age. It is hard to negotiate with this native. Fluctuating relationships seen regarding closer family as well as distant relatives. Only when in the mood, he would mix with them all. On the other hand, he would totally withdraw from them all. Mental levels can be very highly intelligent type to someone with learning difficulties. It is hard to guess their mental performance from outside appearance.

RETROGRADE MERCURY OPPOSITE RETROGRADE SATURN

Very serious thinking or at times quite limited mental usage seen here. Self repressive tendencies, uncommunicative nature, or just introversion likely. Speech and learning difficulties can be potential here as the native has unusual challenge in disciplining his nervous system. Hearing loss or low audio response can be noticed as well with uncommon means of expressions. Life is taken very seriously and lived slowly in terms of events. Thus, the native may feel like experiencing life in slow motion. Good events remain good over a long period, whereas problem areas do not disappear quickly. Reflection process is hampered. As a result, feedback reactions from others and foggy objectivity are noticed. Job and career wise there are always stresses. Career could be good but the work very dull in it. Services are often compromised in profession along with compromise of ego on the job. Thus, the native may not think highly of his work-profession areas. Some sort of mental weakness, problems or weak mental health is noticed. Problems with brother/sister relationship seen here, if not, lack of them can be likely. Sexuality and sensation suffers, making it hard for him to have good relationships. Conflicts of interests as to what the profession can be and what he likes to do. In the educational matters, he has to take it slow and easy. However, within himself he may be much smarter than others give him the credit for. Self-confidence can be lacking here as the native has hidden phobias about his externalizing. Morbid thinking, lower and distorted sense of purpose noticed. Delays in travel or communicative frustration seen. Learning and relearning lessons from the family and nearby surroundings noticed. Father and mother's side of the family cannot get along here causing conflicts between the parents.

RETROGRADE MERCURY OPPOSITE RETROGRADE URANUS

Considerable nervousness and constant thinking process are noticed here. Innovation tries to dominate simple logic but ends up being dominated by logic. Here it starts off with a simple idea but the need to improve the idea grows. The individual has a hard time deciding whether it should remain a simple idea or a perfect innovation. He fights within himself to out-do himself. At times the fight may be aroused to bring simplicity into his thinking. Ultimately, it becomes too late to apply what he thought of, so the confusions and nerves take over the entire story. His indecision or uncertainties are his worst enemies. Communication imbalance is seen here. Either he shows a lot of communication or nothing at all. His mind may be sharp, brilliant, innovative, and inventive, but he has to learn the discipline, patience, and decisiveness. His brilliance may fluctuate in life. Thus, if he is smart in his childhood, he fades away soon and vice versa. Speech may be too fast for others to comprehend or his internalizing is very slow compared to others. Environment and nearby family exerts unusual pressures and influence upon this native. As a result, learning has to be done on a self-sufficient level rather than on a one-to-one basis. The school system does injustice to this person. Many ups and downs or periodic changes are noticed in work situations. There is a unique but distorted sense of services here. Friends on the job can be his real enemies or competitiors. Diet and eating habits can be very strange as the digestive, intestinal system is different and some problems may be evident. Attack of nerves, need for mental independence, and communicative suppressions are possible. Even though, he becomes a victim of his ideas, thoughts and communications, he must cultivate and learn from them. A complex brother/sister relationship is possible along with a very nervous temperament in travel or motion. Reflexes are very unusual, sensitive, and even periodically distorted. Verbal battles, disagreements, or mental combats with friends and group association are noticed. Due to nervous distortions, the proper release of inner pressures is certainly needed for this individual periodically.

RETROGRADE MERCURY OPPOSITE RETROGRADE NEPTUNE

Mental confusions, uncertainties, and dislocated thinking are quite possible in this situation. Subjectivity-objectivity reversals occur abruptly and bring procrastination, delays, or insecurity to one's decision-making power. Logic and instincts fight within, with uncertain last minute outcomes. The native has a hard time sticking with pure reasoning or just going by the "gut" feelings. No matter which he prefers or chooses, the other choice hounds him later. Mental creativity, fascinating ideas, psychic communications are significant. However, the native has many inhibitions and hidden inferiorities of his true capabilities. Thus, he may not be well thought of by himself. Work appears confining, but he performs well under isolative environments. He does not like to brag about his assistance and services to others but at the same time, no one explicitly credits him for his efforts. His frustrations converge very well to elevate his life philosophies. His knowledge may not have the depth, but his reasoning power provides him with enough answers. Excessive thinking is likely, causing substantial inner nervousness. Periodic release of the inner nervousness is needed in order to avoid potential breakdown in this case. Unusual problems in travel or just mere confusion in motion is noticed. Fantasy and escape tendencies are crucial to his well being as his tolerance to circumstantial pressures is quite limited. Sensitivity and reactions to environments cultivate excellent psychic tendencies, but he may not be able to use them for himself. Disillusionments, deceits, or misunderstandings through brother/sister or through the family of either parents are quite likely. He needs to be careful of this situation. Physical health requires attention as his symptoms are either hidden or immunity to certain medicines is possible. Some mental kinks and abnormalities can be feasible to this native, and his communication-learning means are very unusual. Symbology becomes more important in the longer run. Nervous disorder or stomach malfunctions are likely.

RETROGRADE MERCURY OPPOSITE RETROGRADE PLUTO

Mental fluctuations and periodic attack of shrewdness noticed here. Planning, arranging and constructing things on an intellectual level are very significant. Constant internal mobilization of mind noticed, but their constructive usage is not very productive all the time. The individual takes pride in mental perspectives and not necessarily in the true achievements. As a result, strategy, game plan, and the tactics can be far away from the actual action. Mental kinks are possible as the person hides himself from his own thinking. Communicative stresses or imbalance in expression quite possible. True mental capabilities and intellect seldom gets reflected. Thus, in actual learning sessions, the individual will not appear as bright as he otherwise would be. Inner discomforts, phobias or feelings of detachments noticed from brother/sisters. In their earlier childhood, they have the need to be isolative or they are somehow left isolated due to circumstances. They need communication exchange, and mental osmosis from others, but are a little afraid to ask for it. Surrounding environment often appears hostile to them. Interest in deep philosophies, psychology, detective/deductive reasoning, psychosynthesis and counselling can be strong. At one time or another, they will get involved in such psychological exchange or assistance. Learning a great deal through proper services, work and business oriented areas noticed. They often have unusual sense of services or unique ideas about work which need to be transcended before they get successful. Suppressed reflexes can be significant, creating chronic physical distress in the mid-body section. Circumstantial detachment or sudden void is created from the mother's side of the family. Once cultivated, writing and communicative skills can be key factors in their lives.

RETROGRADE VENUS

Emotional hesitancy or indecisions noticed in the native in this case. For some reason, he has difficulties expressing his true emotions consistently. Thus, he would show happiness much before or later, the actualization of the situation. This delayed response or inappropriate expression appears quite different to others. As a result, their opinions about this individual will vary substantially. To some, he would be appearing insensitive, stuffed, egocentric, self-passioned or snobbish. The unusual mannerism or treating surrounding people the way he does may not be done intentionally. His own insecurities force him to take cover of something he is not. On the other hand, when he is confident of himself, he over-compensates his response and thrusts upon others his emotions and feelings. The native can be very hard to please under normal situations. In certain cases, he may be so easy to please that others are doubtful of his games and motives. The distortions in the emotional fluctuations bring the femininity out. In a man's case, this represents inner doubts of his own sexuality and at times his competitions with a feminine woman turns into mild chaos. As a result, he needs a strong woman or power behind her to keep him interested in her. The imbalance of this introvert, easy going masculinity forces him to undertake easy projects, goals, and creative achievements. Personal needs and expressions become very soft, adaptable and fanciful here. Fond of art, creativity, music, comforts, foods and excessive indulgence can be seen here. General appreciative moods and peace loving character visible here. Rather than going after goals, he waits for the right opportunities. Financial success, marital happiness and partnership bliss can be there for him. However, periodically he withdraws with feelings of self inadequacies and this causes frustrations in his life and subsequently in the partnership. He avoids trouble at all costs as he prefers peace and harmony around him. In financial areas, he does not have to struggle hard for simple necessities, but to prove him worthy of his character, he goes out and asks for struggle in life. In a woman's case, her femininity can be very strong but she has doubts of her own from within. They come from her interactions with others and not being able to be pleased by men easily. Her finicky attitude, self love, self indulgence and high satisfaction quotient makes it hard to live with her but tough to get away from her. She is willing to give up true love and romantic idealism for the sake of material comforts, sensuous pleasure, and physical satisfactions. Very jealous attitude towards her spouse might be seen as she demands a lot of attention from him. In early life, she wants to be treated like a princess no matter where her life origin may be.

RETROGRADE VENUS THROUGH THE HOUSES

Retrograde Venus Through the First House. Likes himself a lot, narcism, easy going, indecisive, pleasure seeking, charmer, withdraws quickly in romance. Fickle, changeable moods, loves the world but cannot concentrate on his affections. Artistic, creative, and talented. Self-image important, expects others to like him, fluctuating femininity, double standards, sensation seeking but fulfills himself, aware of self-magnetism and diplomacy. Looks overtake everything. Needs to be identified at all costs, crowd chooser rather than being chosen by others. Love of display, quiet beauty but dynamic appeal.

Retrograde Venus Through the Second House. Financially lucky but opportunistic, exploits money, values, pleasure, and beauty. Things come to him without serious efforts. Losses and gains through women, femininity and glamor. Financial security expressed in terms of visible assets and holdings. Good voice, expressions and poise, preserves himself well, uses others for his gains, confidence in his values and worth. Great upturns in finances. Luxuries, lucrative living and credit crunch wipe him off. Pleasure valued substantially. Materialism and sensuousness.

Retrograde Venus Through the Third House. Soft spoken, charming communication, good voice or expressions, excellent body language, pleasurizes through ideas, fond of travel and things in motion. Takes an easy way out regarding learning. May cheat in education but gets away with a cute grin on his face. Dimples protect him, may not be smart but appears educated. Sophistication projected, good manners when he is in the mood. Likes exquisite surroundings, gains and losses through brothers/sisters. Habit formation.

Retrograde Venus Through the Fourth House. Domestic luxuries, fond of mother or her pet child, enjoys domestic solitude, gets high on his domestic surroundings. Accepts family tradition without causing rebellious tensions. Support from the family is seen. Good home keeper, motherly instincts, industriously creative at home. Weak life foundations, does not like to make key decisions at home allowing the spouse to control the relationship. Being a mama's child causes future dissatisfactions. Hobbies, creativity and talent at home. Fond of nurturing others without responsibility, insecure in actions.

Retrograde Venus Through the Fifth House. Romantic, easy going, pleasure loving but noncommital, butterfly attitude, touchy nature, sensitive reactions, creative, artistic, and talented. Sense of living more important than purpose. Loves children but may not enjoy responsibility. Financial speculations bring lucky gains but eventually he breaks even. Self-love, self-admiration, fond of father or liked by him. Introspective and attention seeking. Demands loyalty but displays fickleness, pleasurism, and indulgive in hobbies.

Retrograde Venus Through the Sixth House. Enjoys work as long as it is easy. Takes job seriously but without responsibility. Independence, uniqueness, and isolative productivity seen. Wants others to appreciate his work, but does not like monotony. Productive but hates production. Conflicts with women workers. Beauty, consumer products, arts, crafts, glamour, industry, photography, music, etc., significant. Romance on the job but frustrations as an outcome. Enjoys rich foods, drinks and services. throat, thyroid, kidney/bladder weakness, beauty inherited from mother's side of family, anti-union on the job.

Retrograde Venus Through the Seventh House. Fluctuating objectivity, easily influenced by the marriage partner, social involvement can be strong at one point and then suddenly detached, diplomatic, indecisive but easy going, love of luxuries and enjoys partnership. Multiple marriages or romantic manipulations. Love of marriage but the spouse demands freedom and independence. Beauty, charm, magnetism, and unique personification seen in marriage that keeps him bewildered. Fragile marital bond needs periodic renewal, fickleness visible due to others. Social image vacillates that hurts in politics or socializing.

Retrograde Venus Through the Eighth House. Preoccupation with sexual ideas just to control the relationship. Sex as a weapon in the situation. True jealousy does not come out. Inner frustrations and self-consumed desires eat the person periodically. Sexual hangups or surrogate situations, bad habits associated with one's pleasurism. Benefits and growth through combined resources but ultimate division of it can be certain. Credit, taxes and insurance claims bring sudden luck but losses through unexpected legalities. Death of a loved one causes emotional breakdowns. Suppressed possessiveness, guilt feelings.

Retrograde Venus Through the Ninth House. Idealism, material richness, general good luck, institutional success, legal benefits due to personal magnetism, problematic second marriage, but the native insists upon that, accepts easy approach to life, difficulty understanding complex philosophies. Success away from birthplace, distant relatives important in life, laziness towards higher education or higher learning. Easy publicity received but bad image can be possible.

Retrograde Venus Through the Tenth House. Weak father image and native finds his approach to success very nonchallenging. Good social status is feasible but anti-social attitude rejects publicity. He often gets what he does not want in life easily. Under pressure he can be timid and finds short-cut in escapment. Age or maturity difference level important in the relationship. Goals are important and means can be immaterial. Success is recognized but not achieved. Ease expected in life, support from his family and in-laws. Romance with power, crafty pride.

Retrograde Venus Through the Eleventh House. Many women friends with or without choice. Competition of the femininity seen. More girls than boys expected, group associations, socializing, women's clubs can be significant. Art group, music, associations, hobby centers and volunteer situations visible. Easy goals chosen in life. Quite prosperous middle third of life seen. Financial benefits through father or his family. Frustrations and emotional trauma from women. Learning lessons through friendships.

Retrograde Venus Through the Twelfth House. Very easy going, indulgive past life, romantic fantasies, self satisfying tendencies, daydreaming, self-disillusionment in romance. Hidden relationships or strange fascinations, gullability towards magnetic people. Sensuous sublimation consumed within, with or without added relationship. Intoxication, unusual turnon's, musical reliefs, creative expressions, enriched subconscious, easy passage to the past, make-believe situations, drama, music, film industry. Karmic relationships and mystical encounters.

RETROGRADE VENUS RULING THE HOUSES

Retrograde Venus Ruling The First House. Fluctuating charm displayed by the native puzzles others as to the real personality of this native. Indecisions are definitely seen here but the native has a way to deal with it using his magnetising powers. Diplomacy, easy going, and poised nature cannot help but like the person. Individual likes and dislikes can be significant, making him very picky about others. His way of showing this can be all tongue-and-cheek type. Unique mannerism with responses to others that are exceptional and sensational noticed here. Self love can be important associated with fashions, glamor, and high living. Individual taste can be slightly out of this world as he creates his unique fashions and perspectives. Fickelness changeable attitudes and moody nature can be seen here. A sense of femininity surrounds the native no matter what his choices and preferances can be. Individual freedom is important and the butterfly attitude visible. Creativity can be superb but individual laziness needs appropriate control. He knows how to get the things done from others. Marriage and partnerships turn him on as long as he is single. However, once married he cannot wait to dream about his individuality, freedom, and independence. This native cannot be bound by any restrictions or commitments as his nice butterfly colors fade away with restrictions.

Retrograde Venus Ruling The Second House. Financial fluctuations are seen. The native may not be happy no matter what he acquires. Material indulgence may oppose his basic personality. However, he tends to be rebellious against his own character. There is almost a hidden competition with spouse regarding the flow and spending of resources. A sense of trade and barter is very crucial in his life. He will use his resources to get what he wants, but later on he will trade that for something else. As a result, his passion for material goods can be fickle and changes frequently. This instability of personal worth forces the native to over-compensate in some areas of life and achieve tangible results. His approach to such achievements will use his exceptional talents, magnetism, charm and utilizing the right contacts. Group associations change periodically, in his life as he can be a sweet talking person but not fulfilling his part of the bargain. In life, he will achieve good material status, but due to sheer laziness may lose a portion of it abruptly. Compassion, sympathy, and supportive emotions shown by him, but he may not actually help others considerably with his efforts. He is willing to part his proper connections, but not the actual efforts to others.

Retrograde Venus Ruling The Third House. Quite charming communication and manner seen here. However, his reactions and opinions can be fluctuating and indecisive. He takes an easy way out of thinking or may be sluggish in grasping things. Learning through his feelings is more important than logic. He is not responsible for his communication as his sweet talk promises more than he can deliver. Fond of travel, no matter where it may be, brings excitement to the native. Pleasant gestures often bring others attention to him and make him popular. In school his charm gets him better grades than actual studies and brilliance. Brother/sister relationship can be very easy going, content and mutually fulfilling type. However, later in life, he gets the compulsion to find appropriate similar substitutions just for fun. Lack of planning and determination gives him soft will to pursue things. Diplomacy associated with internal rigidity helps him become a good sales person. When his sales ability fails, he takes the cover of ignorance and becomes the devil's advocate to fulfill his sales-pitch towards success. Good humor seen in him, but he can be sympathetic towards a bad joke teller.

Retrograde Venus Ruling The Fourth House. Domestic comforts and a lot of artistic, creative, and decorative influence at home is significant here. The native wants pleasure and indulgent surroundings for his living situations. Roots of life are loosely planted giving him a chance to reestablish anywhere else when he chooses to. This domestic flexibility or lack of rigidity comes from his life attitudes. "Home is as comfortable as one makes it" can be the motto. He wants peace, quiet, and unwritten discipline at home. His early childhood can be full of luxury, ease, and freedom. Not being able to satisfy himself under any conditions makes him a spoiled child. In a man's case, he becomes the mama's boy and given a lot of concessions and privileges. However, later in life he resents that treatment as it spoils him psychologically. This motherly over-shadow hurts his masculinity and self assertiveness. In a woman's case, she always tries to out-do her mother or turn worst than her. Domineering father's influence highly noticed here, even though mother keeps him under control using her magnetic sensation. The native is not very sure of his family roots and traditions and how they actually affect him. Real estate and property benefits can be important here.

Retrograde Venus Ruling The Fifth House. Quite romantic, idealistic, and pleasurizing nature seen. However, the native can be indecisive as to what he wants in the long run. Emotions fluctuate or vacillate frequently creating more than one interest in the personal life situations. It is very hard to say "no" to others as his soft spoken, sympathetic and tender side does not like to hurt them. As a result, he involves in situations as they come without being discriminating and selective about them. In a man's case, he can be very touchy, sensitive and fragile emotionally, putting his heart over his head in most situations. A radiant leakage of his feminine side allows others to take advantage of him. Subsequently, he gets frustrated by his romantic interactions and changes his intentions in the long run. More daughters than boys seen as offsprings to this native. With children either he likes them and they do not, or vice versa. As a result, one way relationship is possible regarding children. Excellent creative and artistic talents are noticed here, but the native does not put sufficient efforts to cultivate them. He likes to take an easy way out without complicating his personal life situations. In a woman's case, unusual interactions with daughters noticed. Over compensatory attention given to them, what the native lacked in earlier life. Speculative luck can be with him but it remains uncertain periodically. As a result, he wins a lot when he expects it the least.

Retrograde Venus Ruling The Sixth House. Very easy going work attitudes seen. The native always wants more compensation for his efforts compared to others. Due to strange luck, he often gets a better deal in terms of work and rewards. His charming laziness on the job magnetises others around him making the time go by faster than usual. Thus, his company is well appreciated by his co-workers. A sense of serious responsibility might be avoided by him on the job, as he prefers group actions to boost the group efforts. Changes in diet are significant as he indulges in good foods, drinks and general excitement. He likes to experiment with things in general as far as the surrounding environment is concerned. In doing so, he gets a better pleasure from the environment and to fit his individual taste. Financial gains and ease from the mother's side of the family can be significant or their closer relationship with the native seen. Problems with sugar/salt imbalance in diet. Kidney, bladder, throat, thyroid or lower back areas need attention. His charm, magnetism and good expressions add to his services as another plus that attracts others toward him. Comfort and security may be felt on the job but due to lack of productivity he may be compromised for another co-worker. In a woman's case, minor behind-the-scene activities happening in her husband's life or added third party interference in her life.

Retrograde Venus Ruling The Seventh House. Marriage partner often requires a lot of freedom and independence. Emotional expressions lag behind the actual events or feelings are externalized much later on. This gives a mild insecurity to the native. Not knowing how the person feels from time to time, creates inferiority within him. Hostilities and anger gather but the spouse can have excellent timing to combat this build-up by overcompensating the emotional interactions. This fluctuating romanticism or emotional tug of war works both ways to unify or disintegrate that relationship. Learning lessons from the marriage-partnership areas can be very important. Social interactions or socializing plays crucial role in his life to diffuse his frustrations. Thus, he will involve himself in many activities at times and then totally detach from them to be a home body. In a man's case, it indicates more than one marriage or he has to learn to accept severe emotional fluctuations in it. Wife appears fickle, unstable or butterfly type to him. In a woman's case, she is highly attracted to a non-macho image, sensitive, artistic & feminine type of individual. Even though, she does not intend to make him a hen-pecked husband, he should have all those qualifications. Social behavior and mannerism in the society can be uniquely displayed by the native. Objectivity fluctuates considerably in this case.

Retrograde Venus Ruling The Eighth House. Inner fight within one's own emotions seen here. At the least, he wants to be possessive, jealous but romantic and idealistic all at the same time. As a result, love and sex create mutually dominating approaches to achieve the objective in personal interactions. The native is not sure, which approach to use or what would satisfy him the most in the long run. Thus, what appears on the surface is much different than what he has in mind. Passionate possessiveness, blind romanticism, crude idealism and intense withdrawals are all seen here. Combined values can be excellent and material growth is achieved through the partnership cooperation. However, under problematic detachment, dividing the combined worth represents the biggest challenge and frustrations of the relationship. Partnership can be beneficial to both as long as mutual demands and expectations are fairly reasonable. In a man's case, women come and go out of his life uniquely, abruptly and strangely. Lessons through females, his interactions with them and dealing with hidden resources are very significant. For a woman, it indicates financially strong or lucky spouse. Marriage and social glamour do not match in this case, as the spouse can be non-adaptable to handle both the fronts. Some reversals in finances or potential hindrance from inheritance noticed here.

Retrograde Venus Ruling The Ninth House. Life philosophies are very flexible and adaptable. Anything that provides easy way out, least complications, and quiet pleasure will be given a shelter by the native. He does not like philosophical responsibility as he would seldom wish anything bad to others. The best combat in this situation is retreat rather than retaliation. He would avoid trouble in order to make everybody happy. His gullibility to others beliefs make him susceptible to quick sympathy. However, he can get out of that burden very charmingly. He is responsive but may not be responsible to others problems. Higher learning or education is pursued if it is not too much challenge to his brains. Idealism, creative pleasurism, and esoteric indulgence can be noticed in him as an escape rather than a way of living. A sense of beauty and comfort attracts him bringing nice travel; possibly overseas, or fantasy vacations. Although it appears he may lose in legal matters, last minute changes help him win the situation. In-laws can be important and beneficial in his life. When applicable, second marriage provides good emotional interactions, easy, comfort and happiness. However, it will not have the stimulation and excitement he had in the first situation. Diplomacy, polite stubborness, and cute criticism help him in the areas of representation, sales, marketing, or communications.

Retrograde Venus Ruling The Tenth House. Good relationship with father or much more sensitive interactions seen with him. In a way, mother could be a lot stronger than the father in this case. As a man, this native slowly feels humiliated from his father due to overpowering mother. In a same fashion, he may encounter dealing with father so easy that it loses its challenge. It is not very hard for the native to take upon his father's similar qualities. Under pressure, he can be very indecisive, confused and sensitive. As a result, he tries hard not to get into that spot. He would avoid professional competition and circumstantial crunch by being very unique, independent and self creative. As a superior, he treats others very well gaining respect from female subordinates. Artistic, creative, talented design, fashions, merchandising, consumer products, beautification areas and glamorous applications are important in his career. Social focus can be highly connected with his professionalism. Although his ego can be weak and touchy, he conquers very well once he feels confident of his domain around him. It is very hard for this person to deal with a female supervisor as the clash of the feminine side disrupts the true working spirit.

Retrograde Venus Ruling The Eleventh House. The native expects a lot of high goals, easy achievements, and comfortable surrounding. However, his achievements change once he realizes the efforts needed for their completion. As a result, he will go for cheap thrills, quick sensations, and moderate accomplishments. For some reason, he is happy with friends who are not the "go-getter" type and feels at ease with moderate success. Friendships here have a lot of material, indulgent, and recreational touch rather than trying to help boost each others life. Sharing of the job and happiness with calm and comfort justifies the friendship in this case. Group participations have social goal rather than high powered individual competition. Benefits through father or his success over-shadows the native. Love-received can be very much in disharmony to the love-given. Thus, the native has no control on how much he is appreciated, admired, or loved by others. All he can do is perform his part or duty and hope for the best. Luck through group associations is likely, especially regarding the entertaining types. Friends come to rescue when he needs them. At times romance and friendships end up being sacrificed by him.

Retrograde Venus Ruling The Twelfth House. Unconsciously or indirectly the native is a material worshipper. No matter what the outside influences appear towards his esoteric/spiritual pursuits, his feet are solidly on the ground, thinking of materialism and how it benefits him. As a result, it is hard for this native to totally withdraw from the earthly desires and wander in the pursuit of true spiritual enlightenment. In a man's case, romantic fantasies, make-believe situations or narcisistic tendencies are significant. Hidden fantasies turn him on so much that real involvements can seldom compete with them. A closet affair or need for a hidden relationship can be significant in this case. The person has a great way of expressing feelings, emotions, and natural urges through indirect means. Self satisfactions and self indulgence may be visible here. He can be emotional, touchy, vulnerable and sensitive. In a woman's case her attractions towards femininity are much more unique and subdued. She requires a soothing comfort from another woman or feminine identity that she cannot satisfactorily get from a masculine person. Very unusual and even abnormal romantic/sexual fantasies seen here. Introversion and feelings turn inwards for self-satisfaction rather than outward expression. Strong creative inspiration and vivid imagination seen here.

RETROGRADE VENUS OPPOSITE MOON

Very soft, sensitive and touchy emotions noticed here. The native is attracted to femininity, introversion, and subdued calm. In interpersonal activity there is almost a battle of emotions and feelings. Both parties try to outwit each other using emotional strength. In a man's case, his feminine side almost matches with his mate's and the outcome of the combination can be excellent at times but very hard to control in general. Too much of the same thing repels each other in this case. However, he is strongly attracted to that type of personality so that he has to face the situation head-on. In a woman's case, she finds her man very insensitive to her and at times competes with her. She certainly is not the type who favors competition with male stigma. In general, emotions are indecisive and often get compromised to imagination. Thus, true feelings are sublimated into something fantasizing or make-believe situations. Marriage is often sacrificed and compromised for the sake of stable home conditions. Life security and roots of life gain considerably more priority over money and partnership areas. Thus, mother gets an upper hand in comparison to spouse or the native allows her interferences in life without resentments. In due time, mother-in-law syndrome is created and the native suffers the most out of that battle. Excellent imagination, sympathetic nature and sense of service nicely cultivated in this case. The person is willing to help others at all times. Sometimes, the native thrusts his assistance upon others just to make himself feel good. Busy body attitude may be displayed as a result of it, but that occurs unconsciously. The native is very sensitive to the surrounding influences and quite apathetic towards others. A sense of repressed humanitarian attitude seen here. Creativity and artistic display work through internal pains and frustrations. Thus, the native brings his best output in reality when his emotions and feelings are truly hurt inside. Seriousness towards pessimism displayed rather than laughing at the face of disaster. Home and property benefits quite significant in his life. In many cases he receives rewards for compromise later in life. Strong idealism towards mother or being an ideal mother can be important here. General indulgence in foods, liquids, drinking, and emotions noticed. Excessive emotional needs may create periodic depressions and let downs, if not properly controlled. Dealing with general public, masses or larger domestic situations significant.

RETROGRADE VENUS OPPOSITE MARS

A sense of sensation fluctuates here as the native is not sure what truly turns him on. Romanticism fights with physical passions and the animal magnetism wins at the end. Thus, true love gets sacrificed and compromised in the line of action or for quick excitement. Artistic, creative, talented personality nicely visible here that magnetizes others quickly. Charm and spark in the personality can ignite quick interactions and attractions. Fond of music, dancing, and active excitement seen here. Whatever the native fantasizes within, for the ultimate idealism he never gets fulfilled but sudden, irrational actions bring equal pleasure to him. A sense of dominance, masculinity or authority overrides deep but soft feelings from within. Thus, the native often resents himself for having so opposite needs of personality. Constant excitement in marriage or personality seen and the native expects the spouse to compromise towards him. Partnership sacrifice is expected from the other person through a graceful act. Multiple games are often played in the interaction. Thus, the native creates situations which instigate voluntary compromise that his partner intends to do, to preserve the situation. Self-orientation is very strong and important to his personality. For that reason, money, marriage, or true love is likely to be victimized. The driving force is strong in the native as he wants to prove himself in the world. There is a charm in his ruthlessness or passion in punishment that magnetizes others toward him. Almost a love-hate combination exists in the relationship. The pain and pleasure association coexists in this situation. In a preprogrammed manner, the native has all the plans laid out to achieve his sensation. At times romantic frustrations drive him to prove himself to be worthy of multiple relationships. Thus, in a man's case, this aspect signifies hurt from a key woman. Subsequently, he needs to take revenge upon the women in his life. He would indirectly drain them of their emotions and feelings without proper respect and reciprocity. His romantic fantasies, and make-believe substitutions can be seriously humorous. In a woman's case, she would expect a mild "henpecked" husband. Her internal needs for superiority come from misdirected or rejected emotions through earlier parts of her life. True feelings are often consumed within as the native is compelled to express a different character outwardly. In spite of the complex emotional nature, his sexual attitude can be very open and of a "no nonsense" type. Physical release of energies can be very important to this person.

RETROGRADE VENUS OPPOSITE JUPITER

Inappropriate emotional exaggeration seen here as the native makes a mountain out of a mole hill in his externalization of feelings. Sensitivity is strong but his reactions can be imbalanced to the situations in his personal life. General indulgence noticed and life can be taken very casually here. Lack of responsibility observed here due to self-oriented attitudes. Me first and others later type of philosophy is important. Financial fluctuations and tensions are associated with personal love romances. Thus, love and money often seem to go in different directions. Happiness from both of these areas can be hard in his life simultaneously. There is tendency to buy love and emotions or place great affection upon the material worth. Enriched family background is quite likely but the native has difficulty maintaining his status in life. Money or resources bring romances into his life, but they become the cause of frustrations eventually. Financial division, value compensation, or distribution of resources are very significant in this case. More than one marriage is quite likely with the second one much more stable than the first one. Somehow the first marriage is sacrificed or compromised for the sake of the second marriage. It could be the high idealism that destroys the situation or at least restructures the same interaction. Legalities, litigations, or publicity associated with money matters and values are seen here that the native cannot get away from. Higher knowledge, higher education, or just the sense of mystical wisdom gain considerable priority over money, love, or marriage areas. His social charm is significant and magnetizing but his mannerism is much different than expected of him. A touch of class that is carried by this native identifies him everywhere. Nothing is too good for him as his taste can be lavish. However, his luck may run out on him periodically thus making him suffocate within for the lack of worldly luxuries. Eventually, he learns the lesson that material happiness is not the supreme type. As a result, his pursuit towards the philosophical unworldly wealth becomes justified later in life. Dealing with people of distant lands, different cultures, or just multitudes of philosophies can be important. Financial involvement, public relations, institutional contacts, legalities, justice, fashion, glamor, religious activities, travel, etc., may play crucial roles in his life. Over indulgence may create problems with weight, sugar, glandular malfunction, liver, kidney weakness, etc. Considerable learning experiences come from his interactions with women, femininity, and feeling reversals.

RETROGRADE VENUS OPPOSITE SATURN

Indecisive feelings and frozen emotions are noticed here. There is almost a fear towards something that obstructs normal flow of feelings. Inhibitions, superstitions, or inner phobias work against the native in expressing his emotions properly. A sense of respect, authority, and superiority override one's feelings. Thus, love emotions are compromised towards maturity or authority. An age difference or maturity level difference is often seen in the relationship. When young, the native gets attracted to older people or someone with power/authority. However, when he gets older, his attractions towards younger nativity becomes stronger. In most cases, the same age group is avoided for different reasons. Attractions towards maturity or trying to provide maturity to someone else is seen here. Relationship with father or domineering parent can be difficult or unsatisfactory. Somehow, it happens due to circumstances beyond control. Thus, the native goes after someone who could fulfil that gap in life. As a result, parental substitute is often seen in the actual relationship. The relationship can be very solid, but it appears cold and inactive to others. Respect has to be achieved and displayed in it rather than normal love, romance and affection. Thus, the feelings are fluid only in the deepest within. In early childhood, feelings of rejection, lack of self worth, and substantial grandparental connections are possible. Career and profession get superiority over marriage and partnership. Thus, marriage may be compromised for the sake of good professional success. Professional status also gains an upper hand over the actual financial compensation. Thus, the native will care more for the true professional image than just making money through other means. Spouse is expected to support the career goals and at times actually helps the native to get there. Rigid, fixed stubborn attitude is seen here that appears as a family trademark. Practical arts, pottery, earthy creativity can be significant. The native shows great respect towards the elderly as he expects the same when he grows older. Family discipline is important but the spouse can differ from the native in its execution considerably. Minor problems with kidney, bladder or urinary system seen.

RETROGRADE VENUS OPPOSITE URANUS

Unusual mannerism can be visible here as the native has special charm or magnetism. Striking unusuality coupled with a touch of eccentricity becomes an asset to the individual. This spark may not be long lasting but enough to get starting interactions with others. Independence is highly valued as the native does not like too many strings attached to his situations. The gypsy attitude is externalized right from the beginning in order not to get caught in heavy responsibility. Serious flirtations seen in love/romance areas as the person indulges in sensation much more than binding pleasurism. Friendships, group associations, or doing things with a larger crowd are preferred over a one-to-one relationship. The native may not be unfaithful but his actions certainly do not declare him innocent. Artistic, creative, and talented side needs a lot of flourishing. As a result, he may indulge in the pursuit of that direction.

Financial fluctuations are significant and subsequently, they are associated with changes in jobs or career. Unusual habit formation can be seen here as the native wants to prove his uniqueness to the person of the opposite sex. At times, the native's habits are undertaken just to punish himself for lack of success in the undertakings. His relationships with others can be very unpredictable, but friendships are preserved with great care. Marriage suffers from his friendships and group involvement. They have to in a way approve of his relationship. He is willing to compromise and sacrifice his resources/values, and material pleasures just to please his friends. Great needs for social interactions, social functions, drama, shows, and unusual displays can be significant. Constant new excitement is needed and the native is willing to experiment. This experimental attitude provides him good inventiveness. Thus, he can come up with good ideas towards pleasurism. When he is not in a mood, he becomes an introvert totally detaching from others. However, in doing so he will still receive substantial attention from others. Impersonal relationships, unconventional involvements, and quite original approaches used in this case. He does not like to go by the book as he creates one for himself. He does not like others to imitate him as he expects his originality to remain so. Trend setting type of personality often emerges out of this aspect that becomes even more unique as the time fades in the background.

RETROGRADE VENUS OPPOSITE NEPTUNE

Strong creativity, vivid imagination and great depth of perception are seen here. The conflict between real and unreal situations can be worth observing as the native submerges in the vast imaginative dimensions. The person likes to complicate his daily activities so that he can find a way to run away from it all. This creation of self-blockage to imprison himself appears masochistic. However, he needs that to fulfill his imaginative powers. Idealism can be to the limit and the native indulges in sacrificing others for his deeper cause. In doing so, he compromises his marriage, values, and worth to get on the top of the rainbow. As a cruel reality, he is disillusioned by the outcome and he goes back to square one. Putting the efforts in creative talents, displays, artistic expressions can be helpful. Anxieties and frustrations are well transformed and converted into superb reality of the unreal world. Escapement tendencies, foggy pursuits, or goals that are not so achievable can be important here. Music, theatrical involvement, dancing, movie industries, photography, glamorous enterprises, etc., can be significant in the native's life. As a child, the native indulges in vivid fantasies and creative expressions. It is hard for the native to know what true love can be as the emotional inflow can be vividly colored. At times, he would even refuse to take things on their inner motives. Thus, in spite of potential deceit, he may just go after things so that he can feel sorry for himself later. Unusual romanticism, hidden crush on someone or getting involved in far fetched impersonal relationship. Spiritual and esoteric growth can be significantly achieved in this life as the native helps others grow along the way of his failures. This fulfillment of Karma is done unconsciously as the native really indulged in life in the previous incarnation. Trouble with women in general or femininity threatens the inner ideology. Thus, in a man's case, other women would be a direct problem. In a woman's case, she may get jealous of other's femininity or women become a challenge to overcome in life. Basically, perspectives towards women are distorted. There is a tendency to be introverted and shy but very rebellious and mischievous nature behind the surface.

RETROGRADE VENUS OPPOSITE PLUTO

Romantic manipulation appears in this case as the true emotions fluctuate with uncertainty. The native feels others are intruding or penetrating into his private, emotional barrier. On the other hand, if others leave him alone, he feels inferior and rejected. As a result, the native is hard to please unless he wants to be pleased by them. Internal conflicts occur between love and sex, subsequently sexuality and physical drive win to keep everybody happy. Giving-in the real romanticism hurts as that can be a big put-down for him. Social life demands considerably more attention than private/homey affairs. Thus, he becomes jealous of the whole world for interfering in his affairs. At times, it is the faut of his spouse who might be a social butterfly or socially attracted. Very sensitive feelings and sudden attack of introversion are noticed in the native. Combined values, assets and together resources have so much more priority than his own worth. At times, the partnership and true sense of sharing are sacrificed for better golden goals to be achieved together. This ideology of long term gains and expansion creates considerable havoc in the short term relationship. There is a limit as to how much he can compromise and sacrifice for the future rainbow. Subsequently, he may be strained beyond his limit of endurance forcing him to leave the scene of anticipated happiness. The basic pitfall lies within the native, as he is attracted to such a strong goal oriented personality. The other person at times takes advantage of his nature. A lack of practicality or knowing what is a great challenge needs attention. Due to his emotional and feeling uncertainties, he is not sure what he wants and who he can have in the close relationship area. Financial cash flow is often at stress with credit and other's resources playing key roles. Often he over extends himself financially just to help others and ends up paying for it in the long run. Problems with sexuality, glamor, social misunderstandings, social disease, and even forceful romantic encounters seen here. Self-loving and narcissism tendencies come about later in life due to unexpected events. Quite different mannerism, poise, and magnetism seen in this native.

RETROGRADE VENUS OPPOSITE RETROGRADE MARS

Tremendous fluctuations in romanticism and sensuality seen here. Love and sex create constant battle within and the partnership suffers from it periodically. The native wants the spouse to compromise and he is willing to compromise as well. However, the timing is quite fragile and uncertain for their compromises, thus creating mutual love/hate situations. The harmonizing element can be out of phase periodically. Thus, love me or leave me syndrome is seen here. Money, marriage, and the self-importance are constantly fighting. True love and romantic idealism try to control the physical passions. Then all of a sudden sexuality becomes wild and the pure love is thrown out the window. This uncertainty as to what has a priority at what time drives the spouse crazy. A male/female imbalance is often seen in this individual. Thus, a male person will compete with a female on certain feminine issues, where as a woman will display masculine outburst temporarily. Certain sexual/romantic unusualities or hangups are potential here. "Henpecked man" or "macho-woman" symbology exists in this aspect. Superb creativity, artistic talent and display of unusual magnetism can be seen. Music, dancing, and all sorts of entertaining areas are prominantly in focus. Impersonal relationships often descend out of this aspect. On one hand the native may want to get involved with multiple characters on real or imaginary levels. On another hand, he would be the point of attraction for many others towards this individual. Frustrations from one-to-one situations degenerate into this category. This multiple situation can be exciting on whichever level of reality. However, it can create problems to the native on the physical plane. Over compensation of one's ego is projected through the medium of love/sex magnetism. Outward sensation and inner tranquility may not be in full harmony. Thus, the native justifies his actions in view of his unfulfilled, unreal, and uncommon happiness. Multiple marriages are very likely. However, the first real thing has a deep imprint upon this native. In search of perfecting his first romantic/marriage situation, the native wanders all around, but he cannot truly find anything as good as what he had before. The experiences and agony to go around in that cycle turns out to be what he truly deserves.

RETROGRADE VENUS OPPOSITE RETROGRADE JUPITER

Considerable financial diversification noticed in this case. Over indulgence is significant at times, but then all of a sudden, financial depletions hound the native. Feelings need a lot of reassurance and the native might overly state his emotions. Taking chances, overly extending himself, and financial risky undertakings are visible. The person will not even hesitate to put his love and money on the line to get the happiness he wants. Comforts, ease and trying to find the unworldly pleasures become his goals in life. Philosophies, standards and beliefs are sacrificed to better his money and marriage areas. Then all of a sudden he changes and pursues the philosophical-ethical path compromising everything else. Thus, in life he will experience great ups and downs regarding values, resources, love/emotions, and true philosophical standards. His relationships and expectations of worth go in much different direction from what he really believes in life. It is hard for this person to decide whether material happiness or spiritual tranquility are the goals of life. As a result, in life he pursues both the directions at different times. Using one to manipulate the other can interestingly be seen here. In a way he feels spirituality can buy material substance or material bliss can be used to elevate one's spiritual level. He certainly learns his life lessons as he goes along. Family is important to him to achieve other things but then he will use other means to attract the type of person he desires. Over indulgence causes some physical over growth, glandular-muscle over-expansion, affected kidneys, liver, bladder areas. Sugar/salt imbalance in diet certainly needs attention. Enthusiasm, charm, politeness, finess, tact, and sweet tongue noticed here. Things happen easily in life or at least they are expected that way. Luck is given more priority over hard, constructive efforts. Dealing with combined resources, other's values, and manpower manipulation quite importantly in focus in this case.

RETROGRADE VENUS OPPOSITE RETROGRADE SATURN

Strong romantic, emotional, and feeling reversals noticed here. The native fluctuates between romantic ideology with practical conventionality. Invariably, his choice of his mate is against what his family expects of him. Thus dealing with people much different in culture, orientation and life level seen in close relationship. This romantic rebellion is somehow forced upon him due to circumstances and his own inadequacies. Sexual introductory offers or total withdrawals in that area are likely. Frigidity can be potential or draining of one's own sexuality seen very fast here. Career and marriage clash, even though both try to compromise towards each other. Thus the native will go after career to please his spouse. In doing so, he will neglect the spouse. On the other hand, he may compromise his career for better marriage; but then the spouse is unhappy due to the lack of financial mobility. Either way he has to learn to balance both simultaneously. In career, there are a lot of open enemies visible and financial fluctuations or uncertain compensations are quite likely. He will try to keep his marriage with good justice and structure, but then his own methods fail upon him. Sudden coldness in the relationship due to high standards and self-pride are seen. Thus, he may not feel comfortable in his compromises but is forced to do so by his inner thoughts. Family and marriage clash, making it hard for him to earn his resources on his own. Thus, he does not get support from either sides. In a woman's case, her expectations from marriage can be substantial and when she sacrifices something in the hopes of getting what she needs, things backfire. Marriage of unworldly trust or simple practical convenient arrangement may be seen here. Kidneys, throat, colds, and thyroid malfunction likely. Great financial variations seen from his family status and his own created achievements. However, he may not have control on that equilibrium.

RETROGRADE VENUS OPPOSITE RETROGRADE URANUS

Unusual romanticism and unique attitudes towards love-joy areas are noticed. Circumstances bring much different attitude to this individual, and his reactions eventually compromise the outside influence. Sensation seeking attitude meets outside opportunities to indulge in a wide spectrum of unusualities. Fickle behavior, emotional reversals, and touchy attitudes can be strong. A need for independence and individuality fight the base desires. As a result, things and relationships last as long as no strings are attached. Extra marital affairs or fantasies towards them are noticed. The individual could also become a victim of the same due to unusual partnership. Little kinky romance, possible abnormalities of emotions or just abruptness of emotional response seen here. Social interactions are highly needed, but not necessarily accepted by him. Excellent art, music, creative talent, along with the ability for innovational self-expression is noticed. Impersonal love romances involving more than just simple one-to-one situations are likely. This native may be highly liked, influenced or magnetized by the masses, and at the same time he needs to draw from their emotional reserves. One way or another, deep involvement with women and learning lessons through femininity are seen. Partnerships and friendships clash forcing the native to be the mediator. Eventually, he may lose them all due to his imbalanced or unjustified blending. Friendships often cause financial events in his life. Somehow, he gets entangled with them and resources in such a way to bring long term unresolved status. Friends and group associations seem to manipulate his values and at the same time he uses values to manipulate them. In a female chart, unsatiable needs for luxuries at all costs are noticed. Glamor, sensation, theater, creative moods, and excellent display of magnetic beauty are seen. Physiologically, the throat, thyroid, kidneys, and urinary system can be very unusual. Substantial financial fluctuations are possible during the life time and even unexpected gains/losses are noticed. Speculative loss, bad habits, or just the need to take a risk requires control. Somehow, he never gets enough love emotions from others.

RETROGRADE VENUS OPPOSITE RETROGRADE NEPTUNE

Romantic, idealistic, creative, and talented personality is well projected in this case. Emotions and sensitivity run quite wild making the individual highly impressionable. Magnetic appeal by virtue of soft and dreamy expressions attracts all kinds to this individual and vice versa. Due to his idealism and taking things for granted, he can be susceptible to false impressions, deceit, misunderstandings, and subsequent frustrations. His personality can be an asset and a liability in a mixed sense. The conflict between the reality and unreality is very vivid, forcing him to escape from situations abruptly. Self-disillusionment is significant and many learning lessons from females and feminity are noticed. Issues of money and marriage are seldom what they appear on the surface. Somehow many strange things or circumstances are involved in his money matters and partnerships. He may feel that he has everything under control and then someone pulls the rug from under him. Behind-the-scene activities can be crucial in his areas of life happiness and indulgences. As a result, his joy can turn into misery instantly. On the other hand, he can escape from tough situations like magic. Drugs, alcohol, or just getting high due to circumstances or surroundings are noticed. A sense of responsibility is very limited, but he takes pride in worldly creations. Creativity for the sake of better pleasure is very important. As much as he can be deceived, he can also be the root of major deceptive projection. More than one marriage is quite possible, and the foundation of such a relationship is very unrealistic and dreamy. Impersonal love relationships are noticed which involve real or unreal components. Self-love as an extra compensation is utilized here. Success in public life is often demanded, but conversely, the native goes behind the curtain abruptly with or without his choice. For some reason he never receive enough love, affection, sympathy, and sensitivity from others. His thirst for that perpetual romance and rainbow of happiness cause him to pass-by many good, real opportunities in life. In certain cases, he can be a far-sighted romantic explorer but blind as a bat for his near environment of reality.

RETROGRADE VENUS OPPOSITE RETROGRADE PLUTO

Romantic or emotional manipulation is clearly seen in this case. Changes and adjustments in one's actual love/romance perspectives are brought about by others rather than him. He depends largely upon others' reactions, opinion, and feedback to determine what is good for him in his personal life. Love and sex dominate each other and he seldom has a choice to just accept one. In other words, love demands respect from sex and sex expects superiority over pure love. The native gets too confused about the issue and either runs away from both or just accepts the package, as is. Cash flow and financial flow can be quite unique and stressful periodically. He may often get involved with other's resources just to get the blame for it. His sensation seeking attitude provides him a lot of excitement in life but he should not expect things to continue smoothly. "Take the things as they come" attitude will be the best one. Dealing with arts, talents, complex finances, group assets, music and sensation oriented businesses are quite significant here. Multiple marriages mostly seen in a man's chart; whereas for a woman, it indicates complex financial battle with her spouse. In most cases, the spouse is responsible for the control of values and assets. As a result, in the battle of love and sex, money becomes the mediator or fringe benefit. Thyroid, kidneys, and reproductive areas need attention due to their weakness in this case. Emotional highs and lows are prominant creating substantial internal stress building. During his life time, he is certainly going to see the extremes in finances, personal worth and life enjoyments. Women and femininity will be the focal point of interests, either way.

RETROGRADE MARS

The retrograde Mars often brings about imbalanced energy flow and energy applications. There is an unconscious discontinuity in expressing one's force and power. Improper temper may be shown by the native. Thus, he may not get mad at things others would very easily. On the other hand, he may have short fuse towards minor incidences. For some reason, he accepts challenges very easily in order to prove himself. Distorted patience may be seen that provokes the native easily. When he has a lot to do, his energies might be wasted in internal friction. However, under unproductive situations, he erupts like a volcano. As a child, he can be a trouble maker, instigator and a great tease. He can be good at initiating complexes within others, but seldom getting the punishment for it. This retrogradation will often get his dirty work done through others. He has to prove his power over others, in order to establish their faith in his abilities. Consequently, he may have to do the daredevil events himself to convince others of his raw energies. He cannot continue to prove himself intensely over a long term. Athletics, sports, gambling, military power struggle with strategy, fire fighting, and other things requiring a sense of masculinity can be important in this case. Mars becomes powerful by way of retrogradation, but not necessarily in good sense. In physical drive and sexuality, pleasurism lags actual actions. Thus, the native feels unfulfilled during the act most of the time, making his partner work harder towards the mutual satisfaction. This out of phase pleasure and action can be visible in him or other directions showing contentment and happiness long after the actions. As a result of this all, considerable fluctuating and changing of sexual needs are seen. In a woman's case, she undergoes a lot of challenges to her femininity and to compensate for it she brings out her masculine side. Competition with men and masculinity is seen. A sense of power, force, authority and dominance are needed in her sexual interactions, even though she strongly resents the person who represents this all. Subsequently, a complex can be created as a result of it. Mars here enjoys the sensation, taking chances without worrying about the consequences and getting high on one's potent strength. Although his individual image may be uncertain, he plays a dual role in life. One being the energetic and macho type and the other being soft, content, and amiable. Challenges through brothers and sisters seen or they stimulate his life considerably. Accident prone tendencies or minor clumsiness seen here. A touch of ruthlessness and carefree attitude seen under his easy going exterior. Rebellious attitude but indirect combat of it noticed. A 'get-even' temperament can be seen but it subsides quickly. He is impatient and rash when he appears calm and collective but vice versa.

RETROGRADE MARS THROUGH THE HOUSES

Retrograde Mars Through the First House. Fluctuating self-confidence, improper expression of show of force, controlled energies, delayed display of satisfaction, late turn-ons but easy cool-offs. Reserves seen but not when desperately needed. Sexual self inhibitions, instigator, accepts challenges, but may not be consistent in execution. Sporty, athletic but sour loser, strange energy strategy used, improper blending of retaliation and retreat, self-fulfilling at times, temperamental.

Retrograde Mars Through the Second House. Financially impulsive but cannot justify spending habits, force as an asset, power valued considerably, worships other's strength but may not be confident of his own power. Misguided or unproductive approach to making money, loss through sport speculation, defective right eye, jealous of resources of brothers and sisters, buys power and influence, good with enemies if they are stronger than him. Values overtake sexuality, tries to prove himself through worth of any denomination, risks taken in life, accidents to spouse, enjoys destruction rather than building.

Retrograde Mars Through the Third House. Impulsive communication, goes back upon his word, achieves verbal strength, display of force more important than its execution, active family life with complex brother/sister relationships, accident prone tendencies or clumsiness in motion, argumentative with neighbors, learns fast but forgets easily, hidden complexes in mother's life, mental approach to sexuality as true satisfactions are distorted, invites arguments but retreats easily, good in mental sports and games, game plan significant but loss through its inconsistent application. Initiator.

Retrograde Mars Through the Fourth House. Active at home, but may not finish his projects. Strong love/resentment combination with mother, dissatisfactions through early childhood but true reality always different than what he thinks. Self destructive to his own foundation. Pleasurism at home demanded, emotional strength expected from spouse where as he provides the sexual depth. Rebellious against the family tradition, impatient and irritable at home, domestic eruptions and accidents.

Retrograde Mars Through the Fifth House. Impatient in romance, fond of sports, athletic, but does not like explicit competition, pleasure seeking without responsibility, strong sense of masculinity that needs to be identified. Takes chances frequently, dynamic creativity, lacks sense of justice, anticipates love/sex imbalance, stress with children or regarding having them, miscarriage potential, distorted female fertility cycle, head strong reactions abruptly shown towards children, constant stimulation expected, objectively blunt towards friends. Spend thrift mother, many domestic changes in middle third of life, irrational gambler but wins unpredictably.

Retrograde Mars Through the Sixth House. Active but fluctuating health, headaches, distorted sense of services, stomach aches, fevers, rash, infections and skin irritations, problem with servants or through their untrustworthiness. Active mother's side of the family, many changes in living conditions at the end of life. Behind-the-scene matters associated with spouse, high strung sexuality or nervous physical drive, argues on the job but can be a good initiator, does not like monotony and repetition, impatient to finish his work, requires active evenings, demands service from the spouse as compensatory love, problems with pets, prone to robbery and break-ins.

Retrograde Mars Through the Seventh House. Stimulating and exciting partnerships, man often looks for a strong woman or gets fulfilled through a domineering partner, conflicts and competition of masculinities seen, impatient objectivity, rash reactions, controlled sexual urges suddenly explode, social misbehavior, dominance through spouse, phobias towards open enemies, mechanical, crafty and articulate, unjustified means, accepts animosity quickly, sudden rise and quick fall in public image, anti-rebellious, self-consuming, retaliates at other's expenses, enjoys daredevil fantasies.

Retrograde Mars Through the Eighth House. Some sexual aberrations with imbalanced confidence, often attracted to people who do not belong in his life, sexual high and low variations cause stresses, sadism and masochism, mutually punishing expectations, mild perversions, problems with credit, combined resources, and other's values, accident prone tendencies, violence, guilt feelings, infection prone, abrupt/explosive situations, financial turn arounds associated with relationships, abortions, miscarriages, or problems with births, corporate difficulties, holds grudges, fear of fire and accidents, resents confinements, rebellious, psychological explosions, fear of interrogations.

Retrograde Mars Through the Ninth House. Impatient in choosing beliefs, success away from place of birth, difficulties through in-laws, sexual inhibitions, philosophically controlled libido, standards manipulate sexuality, sexual rebellion, strong opinions regarding international activities, fights for the country, competes for beliefs, problematic third child, diffused optimism, uncertainties in higher education, military justice, law enforcement or legal battles, dynamic second marriage, bad publicity for abrupt irrational actions, fighting spirit.

Retrograde Mars Through the Tenth House. Strong career orientation, fights for ego identification, vicious under pressure, strong father image, love-resentment with the key man in life, stiff sexual ego, sadism associated with physical pleasures, attracts strong spouse, resents dominance outwardly but enjoys it internally, ambition and actual efforts out of phase, over-achiever or under-achiever, lacks perceptions of goals, gives in to the authority of the opposite sex, late marriage or multiple situations, sudden down fall in public office, many changes in career in early life, instigator, competitive and sporty.

Retrograde Mars Through the Eleventh House. Fluctuating friendships, goals given up easily, always in search of new pursuits, temperamental and self-disruptive, nervous and high strung, problems with offsprings, marital frustrations in later life, sexual awakening through other's experiences, hazards in love received, friends are allowed to control the life goals, rebellious towards group associations, good leader but he does not like anyone following his format, frequent changes and modifications in career in second-third of life, friendly relationship turns serious, involvement and sensation through friends expected, resents material ideas of father.

Retrograde Mars Through the Twelfth House. Constant strategy behind the scene, violent dreams, sexual abuse, sexual fantasies significantly sensational, psychic influences, past life encounters, sexual submissions to the spirituality, hidden affairs under the cover of anything else. For a woman, secret relationships or closet affairs, misguided commitments, war games, secrecies and military combat, daredevil, underdog appeal, hazards through institutions, combative past life. Karmic liability in this life due to sexual misuse in the previous life time.

RETROGRADE MARS RULING THE HOUSES

Retrograde Mars Ruling the First House. Native often under-estimates or over-estimates his capabilities and energies in this case. This fluctuating and indecisive energy spectrum can play games with the person. Thus, he may show great strength and power when defenseless or pretend timid, when he is full of offensive capabilities. In a way, he has a lot to learn about his own strength, stamina, temper, and decisive aggression. Self-confidence fluctuates here needing appropriate complimentary partnership. He believes in his fist power, but the same power can turn against him. In a sense being too powerful for himself or undermining his own strength are seen. Sexuality and physical passions fluctuate considerably from very high to very low libido levels. Unpredictable temper seen here causing the native to explode on minor incidences but keeps his cool for major occurances in life. Athletics, physical fitness, military game plans, fire or chemical involvement, etc. can be significant. Then all of a sudden the native turns completely around and totally withdraws from those interests. Macho image is significant here, by being one, or trying to achieve it. Restlessness, impatience and rash decisions need control. A sense of purpose is compromised for the sake of actions. A lot of energies can be turned inward and satisfied on fantasy levels. Personal indecisions force the native to count upon the last minute actions.

Retrograde Mars Ruling the Second House. Reversals in impulsiveness regarding money matters and spending habits seen. He can be quite active but irrational in his use of values. He derives sensation out of spending rather than what the product can do to him. This impulsive buying potential gets bad under stress or crises situation. There, the native just wants to expend his resources in order to find some internal relief. Actions and excitement are of great value to him. As a result, he may even get into sport speculation without strong success in his return on investment. When his resources are gone, he can be very impatient and he might do every irrational thing. Taking risks, chances, or not showing proper patience towards material things can be his crucial learning experiences. 'Money can buy pleasure' attitude seen here and the native tries to prove his strength by virtue of his buying power. Sexuality can be closely connected with his concept of worth and value. Thus, sex and money become important objectives in life. However, they also become his worst drawbacks in terms of dissatisfactions. In a woman's case, this might be more significant as her libido may be converted for constructive use to build better resources. Thus, she may sacrifice one for the sake of another. Thus, strong interest in physical drive will compensate her money needs and vice versa. The transition occurs sometime in the mid life.

Retrograde Mars Ruling the Third House. Argumentative nature and mental combat seen here. The native loves to pick on others or expects communicative stimulus. Fast and sharp thinking can be noticed but he can equally change his mind easily. The relationship with brothers/sisters can fluctuate from strong ties to uncommunicative detachments. Mental alertnes plays a key role in his life and a lot of sensation is achieved on that level. He will argue on his behalf that he does not like to argue. Inner compulsions for actions and thinking dominate each others. Thus, very inconsistant blend of those two seen together. His bark can be worst than his bite and vice versa. However, it is hard to predict which is stronger at a given time. Minor delays, sudden changes or clumsiness in travel or motion related areas seen here. Slight recklessness is noticed and it comes out when frustrated. If he can grasp and understand the issue first, he will retain it and learn very well. However, when he repeats the same thing, it confuses him more. Thus, over studying needs careful attention in his learning. His handwriting will show fast strokes and he may even skip a portion of it periodically. In the same fashion, his communication or lip movement may be out of phase with actual speech pattern. He can be adventurous in travel, only when he accepts that as a challenge and not in normal situations.

Retrograde Mars Ruling the Fourth House. Quite active early childhood seen here. However, the native feels rebellious towards his upbringing. Although he had a lot of freedom, he resents the home environment. Mother or inactive parent has strong influence upon the native but mutual hostilities remain dormant in the interactions. In a woman's case, she may have to compete with mother. Sexual appetite, domestic excitement and events around the native are very significant in keeping the person happy and secure in life. For some reason the person does not care to follow the family tradition or nobel footsteps of the parent but rather pave his path in life independently. Need to change domestic living conditions, disrupt the life foundations or create new environments around him are important here. Domineering mother or her influence upon father can be seen. Truly the father allows this as he is not so sure of his spouses strength. Complex situations involving in-laws are significant. Here it could be his actual in-laws or his parents vs. spouse cause challenges. Danger of fire at home due to neglect can be likely or the native prefers dry environment at home. His argumentative nature towards the family members is just a way to show affection and attention to them. A sense of tease turns him on quickly to get others ticked off for a short while.

Retrograde Mars Ruling the Fifth House. Inner conflict of love against sex seen here. Delayed response of satisfaction causes abrupt feedback from the other person. Romantic exterior demands raw physical intensity from inside or outward expression of physical drive actually expects romantic idealism. The native takes a lot of chances in love/romance areas and subsequently finds a lot of lessons to learn. His impatience towards children can be seen here. Romance may be used to get to children or children become the stepping stones to get to the heart of another person. Temper tantrums and sudden explosive moods shown towards others in the close relationship. Difficulties in lower education or discontinuities can be likely in it. His mind may not be on the studies or he lacks patience for serious studies. Pleasurizing the physical, athletic, or sporting activities are important in his life. His irrationalism may cause him to take a beating in speculation or risky projects. The creativity displayed by the native can be very dynamic and in some form of art in motion. In a woman's case, the sexuality can be a problem in romance as it may be hard for anyone to satisfy her. This could be physical or psychological but others may feel some frigidity or over expectations. If she desires children, she may have difficulty having them. On the other hand, they happen when she least expects it. Some problems, difficulties, miscarriage potential, etc. are likely. The native wants to treat his children much differently than he was treated as a child.

Retrograde Mars Ruling the Sixth House. The native has a lot of energy, enthusiasm and active spirit in the job. However, he needs constant but varied excitement in it. If he is not active enough on the job, he simply looks for another opportunity. Physical labor, production activities, dealing with metals, fire, machines, athletics, sports related areas can be important on the job. Taking risks or chances on the job are almost noticed here. He is willing to accept the challenge in it but he may not be always properly compensated for it. A sense of adventure, excitement and beating the odds get his attention fast. If his job does not turn him on, he will be quite restless, impatient, and high strung just to do the monotonous things. Work habits can be very active, fast-paced and non-methodical. He has to prove his macho or authoritative image on the job. For that reason, he is willing to use any strategy or game plan to achieve the objective. Clash with superiors can be noticed frequently. Resentment towards any authority or bossy superiors cause disruptions in the job-service areas. Weaker health due to over exertion, high fever, headaches, or head injury potential seen. How to use his head properly on the job becomes a big dilemma here. His impatience can be a virus and contagious to others around him. Sudden attack of nerves, explosive tempers, high blood pressure are likely. A lack of sense of humor on the job or poor sporting spirit seen. Considerable clashes with mother's side of the family seen.

Retrograde Mars Ruling the Seventh House. Constant excitement in marriage expected by him. Spouse can be either argumentative or the native creates fighting situations here. One way or another stimulation is needed for him. He gets what he deserves in worst cases as the spouse can often do a number on him. His normal romantic, easy going, diplomatic personality can be indirectly instigating to make his spouse bring temper out. Learning and relearning experiences from marriage are definitely seen. Complexities, combative mutual behavior but sensational sexual relationship feasible here. In a woman's case, her husband has difficulty relating with her properly or he can be too macho/masculine and forceful to her. This forced interaction can create explosion of tempers, sadistic, masochistic behaviors, and at times mutual love/hate interchange. No matter what, the native enjoys the relationship and sensation associated with it. For a man, the woman he attracts can be very strong, assertive, and dynamic. Almost a henpecked husband might be made out of him in that marriage. In that case, a competition of masculinity or sensation caused by mutual masculine elements is worth noting. General objectivity toward others is indecisive, irrational, and temperamental. As a result, fluctuating social interactions seen here. As an individual, he is liked by all. However, he and his partner form much different personality to be accepted by others on a continued socializing basis.

Retrograde Mars Ruling the Eighth House. Some sexual abnormality can be very likely in this case. The unusuality can be due to mismatch of the partnership rather than individual fallacies. Sexuality needs are not properly expressed, fulfilled and reciprocated here. Delayed response of the pleasures drives both people to be concerned about each other's potential. Fluctuating libido, guilt feelings, extreme frigidity may be seen here. Forceful interactions or sadistic/masochistic attitudes are associated with the physical relationship. Combined resources may create conflicting situations in the partnership. Somehow impulsive spending habits or wasting of common values seen here. The native's impulsive, irrational and risky behavior takes him very close to death or close calls can be scary to others. He may have a difficult time keeping secrets as he loses patience fast. Occult beliefs are fluctuating and he cannot rationalize them in his mind. Hidden activities, underhanded deals, or mildly sneaky involvements can be potential. Problems of credit, insurance, taxes, or corporate group resources need careful attention. Marriage partner can be very different from this individual in many areas of comparison. Quick and abrupt departure from life can be possible along with danger from fire, chemicals or irrational actions in motion. The native appears much too conservative to seek intense actions as pleasurism and sensation in life at all costs. Unexpected benefits through inheritance are likely but then they deplete equally fast.

Retrograde Mars Ruling the Ninth House. The native is very bold, blunt and aggressive in his philosophies and beliefs of life. An impulsive faith might be shown by him but when he realizes the true story behind it, he can be mad and vicious about it. Mild temperamental racism lies within him that draws quick conclusions regarding people and their origins. Excellent grasp on higher philosophies, knowledge and wisdom might be shown by him. However, he can be changing his opinions and faith abruptly and periodically. Lack of patience and persistance may keep the native away from higher education and institutionalized learning. He makes a nice, blunt and courageous spokesperson. The native can be impulsive towards relocating to other places but once he gets there, he cannot wait to go somewhere else. This itch gets to him periodically but circumstances and career hold him down secure most of the times. His sensational needs are not often fulfilled by his profession, so he fantasizes a lot to relieve the internal frustrations. When applicable, second marriage can be very active, stimulating but requiring test of the mutual wills. Distant relatives or people away from home abruptly cause conflicts in his life, but he enjoys them as challenges. In legal matters, sudden reversals of the judgements likely. Thus, simple litigations turn into counter litigations. Some hidden phobias often hound his father or he goes through behind-the-scene involvements with frustrations.

Retrograde Mars Ruling the Tenth House. Under pressure, this individual reacts very agressively and violently, but he misestimates his attack. He likes to take law and order in his hand for the sake of his own justice. The justification given by him can be irrational and impulsively constructed. Very strong father figure is noticed or deep fears and resentments towards him are likely. Power of the will is unexpressed and uncontested in this case. Others are not sure of his potency of strength as they just have to take it for granted in estimating it. At home, he can be very easy going, charming, polite and good host. In business and career, he wants to be a go getter or pioneering type. He can administer well, but only on a small scale. Under mass attack, he is not so well put together. Stage fright attitude can be possible in front of large crowds but a smaller one he can handle very well. He creates his own responsibility and goals. However, he prides in breaking his own achievement records. In a woman's case, dealing with the business world is thrust upon her all of a sudden. Her masculine side comes out to compete with others. Sexuality or physical drive is converted to sheer ego of achievements. As a result, she has to fantizise to extract her own pleasurism. Unusual marriage and subsequent responsibility are seen in her life.

Retrograde Mars Ruling the Eleventh House. Friendships are the proving grounds in this native's life. Changes and sudden terminations seen with his friendships and group associations. He expects a lot of actions, excitements, and stimulations from them. Willingness to give a lot towards friends seen here, but his romantic ideology may not be appreciated by them. Thus, romance and friendships do not necessarily go together. In his group associations, he wants loud voice and a substantial follow up behind him. His so called friends are around him but may not stand behind him on certain issues. Subsequently, hostilities gather and he takes his friendship business elsewhere. His goals and hopes of life can be impulsive and ill-planned. It could be that they are planned too well but executed with haste. Thus, he has to modify his goals periodically taking into account his failures and frustrations. Socializing, glamour, and outside events are important to him but his career can drag him in another direction. Clash between his brothers and father is quite likely. Unexpected separation, detachment, or psychological void from family may be seen. Father's financial impulsive habits get to him as they both differ on the issues of spending and values. In a woman's case, sexuality and personal pleasurism are highly connected with friends, but substantial sacrifices associated with it.

Retrograde Mars Ruling the Twelfth House. Hidden strategies, behind-the-scene matters or some underhanded activities can be significant here. Past mistakes often catch up with him, giving him a phobia of the past. He hates isolation, confining situations, and loneliness. However, his own punishments just put him in those positions. Quite active past life was noticed associated with military, war, criminals, prisonments, etc. His nightmares reflect those things periodically. In this life, he has to learn to be calm, patient, and easy going. Achieving control on temper, irrationalism, and head strong behavior can be his greatest achievements. Under isolative or confining conditions, he gets very itchy, nervous, rebellious and irksome. He likes to be with people and on the job he prefers working with many around him. Sexual discomforts, fantasies, and vivid dream fulfillments seen here. Compensatory mechanism works very hard in this case to convert sexual energies into productive life goals or spiritual pursuits. Learning to control his libido can be important to him in the long run. However, he cheats periodically with hidden involvements through real or fantasy means. Detective, investigative talents are seen here as he can be good at covering his tracks most of the time for a short while only.

RETROGRADE MARS OPPOSITE MOON

Moody, high strung, and temperamental behavior seen here. Emotions are touchy, volatile and abrupt in nature. Feelings run high and low abruptly. Home or domestic security is highly in focus and important to this native. For that reason he may break his own back to achieve it. Strong domestic possessiveness seen here. This over protective attitude really helps the family but outside of the home may be a little miserable. Problems with mother or women in general seen. They are needed but he cannot stand them and this creates the dilemma in life. Relationship with mother can be very touchy and full of hostilities. Being a mama's boy, might create insecurities and incompensation of adequate feelings through early childhood. Constant attention was needed but he hated that when it was thrust upon him. Frustrative moods are created as a result of it. Somehow, he never got a chance to prove his masculinity and male image due to his mother. Her overbearing creates a deep impression upon his subconscious through early years. In a woman's chart, rebellious nature towards mother begins very early in life. Somehow she gets controlled by her mother. Emotional manipulations occur between them and the person feels obligated to do things mother expects or demands. The person at times neglects her own passions, sexuality and happiness to please her mother. Then she hates herself for allowing her to do so for her mother. Getting emotional comforts and reassurance of feelings at all costs noticed here. Her sexual supressions or sexual over indulgence depends upon the emotional security in her life. That is truly her goal and objective. Dealing with older but active woman can be significant in a man's case. Here unconsciously he is looking for the same mother figure replacement, so that he can be fulfilled emotionally as well as get-even with her for any residual hostilities. Quarrelsome nature or argumentative tendencies around the neighborhood seen here. Rash, infections, fever, allergies, and periodic malnutrition noticed here. Hot headedness needs attention as the native does not know what the consequences of his actions can be in the future. Water sports, swimming or relaxation near water can be important in this case. Stressful puberty with difficult monthly periods seen in woman's chart.

RETROGRADE MARS OPPOSITE SUN

Very exciting, aggressive but unstable nature seen here. Attention seeking mechanism is strong but it works on a negative level. Thus, the person gets in the lime light for doing things he did not really want in the first place. Accepting challenges are very easy for him. Anyone can entice him to do certain things as long as that is phrased in the format of challenge. To prove himself at all costs can be his downfall in life. In love/romance, he is willing to sacrifice himself and adapt to various compromises. Creativity can be dynamic in nature or his talent in the areas of action and movement very excellent.

Physical exercises, dynamic behavior, athletic, sports, gymnastic, military, etc., can be important in the life of this native. In doing so, he still has substantial energy reserve within him. He makes a worst enemy as when he competes, he totally disregards his safety and himself. Learning lessons through one's irrationalism, impatience and over exertion seen here. In a woman's case stronger sexual feelings are noticed. She actually competes with the man in every area of life. The macho-femininity attracts a lot of friends and "buddies" to her, but not necessarily the true romance. In personal situation, she expects the dominance, authority and force from the man. However, outside the house she has opposite tendencies. This fluctuating male/female counterpart within her creates insecurities periodically. Clash with father or authority seen here. However, the native respects and abides by them and even sacrifices or swallows the temper. Accident prone tendencies, clumsiness in motion, or simple energy imbalance seen here. Strong determination, goal orientation and will power are well visible. The native will go after what he wants and he will have a great shot at it, no matter if he fails in doing so. Persistence, fighting spirit, and combatic instincts help him get through life with one piece. A chip on the shoulder is associated in this combination. Great sense of respect and admiration towards his children seen, especially in various areas of physical display. Many of the opportunities he did not have in early childhood, will be made available to his next generation. He will make sure his sons are not deprived of any opportunities and chances in life. Taking chances in speculation are visibe here with minor gambling tendencies. Pleasurism and constant exitement are important. In a woman's chart, she may sacrifice her sexuality to please her father.

RETROGRADE MARS OPPOSITE MERCURY

Mental brightness, sharp thinking, and acute mind are seen here. However, a lot of quarrelsome tendencies and mental combat are noticed. Actions and energies are compromised for the sake of better plans, ideas, and strategies. As a result, barking is much stronger than the bite in the combination. Energies, anger and temper are suppressed within, with more scope for verbal or communicative relief. Internal frustrations can be nicely converted to outward expressions, writing, teaching, or mental strategies. Mentality and mental attitudes overtake actual physical actions. Thus, sexual satisfactions are compromised on a mental level. Here the ideas and what to do is considerably more important than actual actions. Physical energies are used only as a threat, but seldom in true reality. Complex relationship with brothers and sisters seen. It is very hard for him to get satisfaction or recognition on the job. Thus, the native gets in the habit of self-sacrifice on the job. Providing communication services, mental approaches, idea unfoldment, business related applications, etc., are seen in work areas. Nerves often gather within, forcing the native to explode suddenly. This appears as an unusual temper tantrum, but instant cool-off is possible. The native may have to compromise himself or take a larger burden upon himself in the family as compared to his brothers and sisters. Stomach problems or weak digestive system can be visible. Sportsmanship or combative spirit is there, but the native has to face fluctuating animosity towards him from others. Complex communicative problems in the marriage or partnership noticed as both work on a diametrically opposite thinking paths. In a woman's case, a brother replacement is noticed in the relationship. Thus, the man in her life has to compete with her brother. In many cases, her actual brother and spouse has a difficult time of interacting, from which she has to learn a great deal. Travel can be exciting and pleasurable. A woman in this case often requires a lot of verbal reassurance for her sexual fulfillment. For a man, he may brag about his masculinity, macho-image or strong physique to get mental satisfactions. As a child this native can be very naughty or mischievous and might get into a lot of minor troubles. The native has excellent verbal conmanship tendency which helps him get in and out of trouble a lot.

RETROGRADE MARS OPPOSITE VENUS

Intensification of sensation is seen here with a lot of romantic or creative expressions. An imbalance in love and sex is noticed that excites the sensuality but suppresses it within. True love or romantic sentimentality wins here most of the time. Self-sacrifice for the betterment of the partnership is important. Here the native values the other person over himself, giving the partnership a boost. Sexual frustrations can be consumed within or projected upon others who are not connected with the relationship. Money, values, and worth are looked at as a promise. For this reason, the native is willing to sacrifice some excitement for it. True feelings rule supremacy over the physical passions. A thing of beauty becomes the excitement, rather than the pleasurism through action. Insecurities, putting oneself down, or self-dilemmas are possible in the interactions. The insecurities are much more significant in the woman's case. Here she is likely to fake her sexual satisfactions just to keep harmony of the relationship. This one sided, male chauvinistic interaction hurts her emotionally, but she learns to live with it. In doing so a stronger male counterpart grows within her personality and all of a sudden she is ready for equal rights, women's movement, etc. Masculine dominance is resented by her but on the other side she wants it badly. This duality of needs and reality tears her apart periodically. Self worth may be in dilemma for this native. As a result, money and values become the tools to prove one's interactions and glamorous excitements are expected by the native but with a shy-sensitive interior. At times, she has a fear towards the outside world, so she pleases the spouse, and eventually, everything is accepted and compromised. Man in this classification can be a "hen-pecked" husband. In any case, a lot of actions, events, and excitement are noticed. Creative potential, artistic, musical, theatrical talent, and super sense of magnetism are seen here. They do not have to act in life, rather they can be on stage constantly. Charm, magnetism, poise, musical/dancing orientation, and excellent sex appeal makes them easy to meet people. Impersonal interactions and mass oriented interests can be significant here. Life is to live and enjoy becomes the motto in this case.

RETROGRADE MARS OPPOSITE JUPITER

The battle between faith and force is noticed here with faith overruling at the end. The force and energies are with him but in the true context of a "show off." Prudence takes over his irrationalism and quick judgements. The native is itchy for action but somehow never gets full opportunity to use his fist. Anger can be spelled out as internal frustrations. Philosophies and beliefs guide his activity in life, even though his rebelliousness goes against them. Establishment of faith and abiding by the standards is taught since early childhood. His own escapement from this all is to run away from the family and authority. In due course, he becomes the authority but not by his force. People respect him for his unused potential and with good faith that he will not resort to power. Ambition is strong and he takes chances with his optimism. His only enemy is his irrational behavior, rash activity, and hard to control temper. Financial, institutional, philosophical, administrative, or legal success can be significant. His ability to look into the future and act upon it with greatest care provides him with good success and recognition. He has to create a track record for others and then he can simply be taken for granted. Potent energies require a lot of physical release, special exercises, sexual openness, and periodic sporty risks. When used with optimum balance of the force and philosophy, he can achieve wonders in life. Higher philosophies, higher knowledge, or elevated subconscious pull him away from mundane practicality. A need to be recognized is significant, but his success comes from others' feedback, rather than his own achievements. At times, he can be very insecure, uncertain, and timid about his own status in life. Thus, two different personalities are visible from time to time. In a woman's case, sexual sacrifices for the purpose she believes in are noticed. Her own satisfactions are secondary as compared to making someone else or something else happy. She can be proud to do this compromise even though it may hurt inside. Once she believes in somebody, that person can totally control her sexuality and libido. Her compromises are fine, but then she is risking to lose her identity. In several cases, woman like this may totally sacrifice her physical drives for the sake of higher esoteric, philosophical or religious pursuits.

RETROGRADE MARS OPPOSITE SATURN

Great self-control is expected or thrust upon the individual. Considerable power play of energies occur within and the native can be an active volcano.

Self-restrictions dominate the indecisive energies with feasible output that is not much productive. The native displays great control on himself but that control is actually circumstantially stimulated. Hostilities gather quickly in this case with a touch of cruelty in the behavior. Sadistic, masochistic tendencies can be common here. Self needs to be recognized on the job, but others do not respect him due to his behavior. Intense competition to be better than his own father is seen all throughout his life, but he may not be successful at that. Indecisions, blunderous attitudes, and serious faulty undertakings require attention. A touch of bad luck is associated here without him realizing the full consequences of his complex nature. Clash with superiors, authority, or government can be crucial that puts him in trouble at the nick of time. In a woman's case, bad marriages or relationships are seen. Actually, ever since childhood there has been a feeling of humility felt. It could be others' appear cruel to her and subsequently, she gathers hostilities towards them. Punishments for wrong reasons, restrictions, limitations, and basic inhibitions are seen. The native feels like combating the situation with all his might, but his uncertainties towards his fighting potential stop him from doing that. Only under pressure will this native resort to force and even minor crime. Social injustice hurts him the most. Self-punishing tendencies, self-sacrifice and self-humility are potential and require attention periodically. Anti-narcissism is seen here due to social withdrawals. Accident prone tendencies due to other's fault are seen. The native has the peculiarity to be at the wrong place at the wrong time. In a woman's chart, sexual malfunctions, unexpected restrictions, frigidity or forceful unions are possible. Key age difference or maturity level imbalance noticed in her interactions. Problems with children or regarding having them can be significant. Dealing with engineering, military reserves, metals, chemicals, or mining areas can be important in career.

RETROGRADE MARS OPPOSITE URANUS

Temperamental attitude with disruptive nature is seen here. The native is restless, nervous, and shaky. Constant excitement is needed or expected with unique outcomes. Considerable electrifying, sparky but abrupt personality noticed here that can be very impressionable to others. Lack of sporting spirit or sour loser attitude can be visible. Holding grudges and reacting on abrupt/nervous impulse is likely. Irrationalism, impatience, and disregard for danger displayed by the native in the hope of being unusual. Sensation can be so strong that he is willing to take a lot of chances to achieve it. Sexuality profile undergoes perturbations. Unusual, uncommon but experimenting involvements seen just to get kicks and satisfactions. Distorted libido and base desires may put him in complex life situations. In a woman's case, this represents multitude of activities with or without choice. Friendships and romances interconnect quite wildly here. Unique sexual expressions, behavior and expectations seen. Men and masculinity are hard for her to understand.

Whatever she does is likely to be taken in another way. Her intents are misrepresented and needs often unfulfilled. Paranoid tendencies due to forceful interactions, physical dominance and masculinity pressure seen in this case. Whether to please others or be pleased by them becomes the classical dilemma. Energy imbalance often puts them in a tricky situation. Hostilities can gather intensely but they may be well acted upon externally. Hypertensions, accident prone tendencies, clumsiness, and distorted reflexes visible. Nothing is done unless it can lead to something unique and uncommon. Self-confidence fluctuates and considerable manipualtive events with friends seen. Sudden separations, detachments, or rejections occur in that type of interactions. Self becomes much too complex and indecisive to be a part of any group association. Going against one's hopes and goals becomes a tradition. Here the native is rebounded from his own expectations and doing something much different than planned or expected. Dealing with military, chemicals, fires, independent services, sports, engineering, high level technology, etc., are significant. Abrupt changes are often expected in life; if not, they are suddenly created by him.

RETROGRADE MARS OPPOSITE NEPTUNE

Instincts overtake the actions letting the native enjoy life on a much higher plane. Make-believe situations, drama, and fantasized creativity supercede actual activity. Energy fluctuations, imbalance, and uncertainties are consumed within to build an excellent creative structure of ideas. Sexual fantasies, make-believe sensation, and substitutive actions are quite prominent here. Escapement tendencies on an imaginary plane are worked out most vividly to provide satisfactions. Getting high on one's own laurels or just indulging in the past is seen in this case. Dealings with medicine, hospitals, spirituality, metaphysical pursuits, drugs, and pharmaceutical areas, theatrical involvement, screen displays, advertising, and any similar make-believe situations very significant in this combination. The native may not be quite certain of his true energies and their long term impact on the projects. However, his sixth sense helps him a lot to project the expectations and judge the achievements on a projected future. Self indulgence, self satisfactions, and self substitution can be noticed. A lot of hidden fears and phobias likely but the native unfolds himself very well in life. Gullability, adaptability and potential deceit need attention. Combative, fighting spirit is overtaken by the higher consciousness. Thus, the native will vividly experience the entire situation first on an imaginary level and then get into its reality. Quite good creative output, imaginative talent, and displays of superb nature seen. In love/romance, idealism fights with true action. Thus fantasies take over real excitement, but the native is happy with it. In a woman's case sexual malfunctions due to hidden stresses or due to past events are noticed. Complicated subconscious fights with the sexual instincts and she has a tough time releasing her potential for optimum pleasure. Thus, periodic insecurities in her indulgive areas are likely. Spunk and zest are quite visible with excellent powers of magnetic attractions. Interests in mysticism, hypnosis, healing, and any energy transactions are very likely. Powers of penetrations, energy expositions, and vivid dreams can be the asset in this case. Complex relationships with men or masculinity are noticed. The native can be unconsciously accident prone or has the phobia to look for such coincidences.

RETROGRADE MARS OPPOSITE PLUTO

Here actions have to abide by the basic strategy. Long term goals require short term sacrifices. Energies are often dragged in to do the work in spite of internal resistance. Inner power-play is substantial and the native becomes the victim of his own energy explosion. Purpose is very important but somehow it remains implicit for the native to concentrate his energies towards. Thus, the native is charged up but without direction or leadership. The internalization of energies or misdirected efforts can be hazardous to the individual in terms of establishing inferiority complexes. Power, authority, sexuality, and potency are very significant factors in determining one's own status in life. The superiority is judged through them and the struggle to establish one identity can be vividly seen. Hyperactions, wasted efforts, and built up nervousness need control. Lessons from patience, persistence, and prudence can be seen here as crucial to the growth of this person. Driving power is considerable and when used properly this native can go places. However, due to built-in self-destructive mechanism, he can explode and become a victim of a heavy downfall in life. Competition, combat and carefree energy usage are seen here. Accident prone tendencies can be potent, if not, things just occur abruptly in his life. Cruelty, sadism, masochism, and temper tantrums are sudden and intense at times. Sexuality malfunctions can be noticed. Here power is used to get his libido fulfilled or sexual energies consumed to achieve power. Due to this, any failure is looked upon as a big blow on his masculinity. In a female chart, it indicates sexual variations, highs and lows and even some forceful encounters. She is often attracted to mean, powerful and strong people. However, she resents their dominance upon her creating strong love/hate combinations. Sexual excess can be seen at times and then turning into frigidity at other times. Needs change so fast that fascination and joy turns into total pain and refusal. It is hard to keep a female like this happy consistantly. As a result, she can become very active in the outside world trying to prove her superiority in the masculine world. Respect for authority is established in the hopes of acquiring such a position of authority.

RETROGRADE JUPITER

The retrogradation of Jupiter condenses its good qualities to a few concentrated areas of life. Thus, overall results will show good luck intensity periodically, rather than continuously. Here the optimism, over expansion, and prudence are controlled by the native due to unknown circumstances. At one point in life, he definitely turns inward to evaluate his philosophies and life values. This inward search soon instigates his exploration of the unknown, metaphysics and spirituality. This awareness of the outside influence of the cosmos upon him, enlightens the inner being but inferiors the ego. Financial fluctuations or changes from one extreme to another most likely seen in this case. If the native is born in an inadequate, limited, or poor circumstances, he will do his best with success to achieve something tangible in life. On the other hand, when born in a rich, materially comfortable state, he will try to explore other areas of interest in life and material pleasurism may not be his priority. Circumstances force him to be less optimistic as his expectations and reality can be far apart. Total changes, modifications, or adjustments in his life philosophies, ethics, and standards are seen all through life. It is hard for him to maintain the consistency of philosophies over a long period due to circumstantial manipulations in his beliefs. In early life, he may neglect the importance of education or give-up easily the opportunity for other life goals. However, as he grows older, he realizes the significance of missed educational learning. As a result, renewal in the interest for knowledge, wisdom, and philosophy boosts later in life. Problems or just circumstantial frustrations through children noticed. In certain cases, this native may not have any offspring or family continuation of his own. Material good luck can be with him when he does not need it. On the other hand, when he expects the resources most, things may turn their backs upon him. Reversals in legalities, litigations, or institutional matters are noticed. Fluctuating publicity or self recognition reversals occur here that he has no control over. Excellent success in various areas of life seen as long as he does not expect it to be long term. Thus, a nine year good luck cycle often maintains in his life. He may have to swallow his pride and ego when things turn back upon him, but he has to take life seriously in spite of his inner compulsions to be happy-go-lucky. Dealing with people of different background, cultures, and beliefs seen here. When applicable, the second marriage can be uniquely different, full of independence, idealistic, and free-floating type. Physiologically, liver, glandular functions, and muscles need periodic attention. Faith in life is often tested by circumstances with periodic rewards for maintaining it properly.

RETROGRADE JUPITER THROUGH THE HOUSES

Retrograde Jupiter Through the First House. Cautious optimism, philosophical reversals, body expansion, idealism with feet on the ground, self limiting philosophies, self punishing attitudes, chances taken for personal goals, subjective attitudes towards children, beliefs compromised for actions, self sufficiency, individual problems blamed for mystical universe, personalized sympathy, carefree but law abiding, travels a thin line between law and disorder, faithful, respect worthy, self-worth reassessed, inner growth for outer achievements, freedom loving but dislikes loneliness, learns by higher consciousness.

Retrograde Jupiter Through the Second House. Financial fluctuations and reversals, money and values drive him towards success, unexpected detachment from material success, faith is valued than the fist, general indulgence, material luck possible with religiousness, praying pays off, happy-go-lucky attitude, problems left untackled, philosophically tuned and mystically attracted, publicity associated with efforts of achievements, financial drain through children or mystical institutions, luck through legalities in combat.

Retrograde Jupiter Through the Third House. Large family background or vast brotherhood, travel and on-the-move attitude, exaggerations, over estimations, promises more than he can deliver, logic and beliefs mismatched in early education, requires a lot of breathing room, inspirationally possessed, mental values important, illogical idealism, takes things literally, fond of knowledge but only on the surface side, supportive of family but it becomes a burden to him, weight and muscle problems in late years, luck through travel and sensational ideas, deep mentality projected.

Retrograde Jupiter Through the Fourth House. Benefits through family and tradition, domestic foundations are important, fond of mother and idealizes her philosophies, luck through land, property or real estate, good upbringing in early life, but his intense needs to explore other beliefs. Roots of life shaken up to judge their deepness and stability. Wide foundations, thorough preparations, emotionally vivid, strength behind feelings, faith in home, takes domestic matters for granted, family inheritance, near sightedness.

Retrograde Jupiter Through the Fifth House. Problems with children or regarding having them, ideology does not go well with children, creative expansion seen, strong faith in own talent, speculative tendencies, learning lessons through risky undertakings, too much or too little pleasures in life, idealistic in romance, takes things and people for granted, displays optimism without sufficient efforts, sudden recognitions and elevations in life. Excellent contacts and influences seen, political interests and international strategies, reversals but eventual success in education.

Retrograde Jupiter Through the Sixth House. Expects too much from the job, idealism in his efforts, self-confusions, means hinder in the goals, under-achiever, large family on mother's side, health problems on grand scale only, pride and beliefs swallowed on the job, good leadership with union connections, services pay off eventually, self-sacrifice needed for success, unexpected good luck in the late years of life, confining work resented, politics on the job, liver, muscles and glandular difficulties, fights for justice for coworkers, attracts religious spouse or the other person can be very esoterically stimulated. Work now, rewards later attitude.

Retrograde Jupiter Through the Seventh House. Late marriage or more than one marriage likely, imbalanced freedom needed by both parties, optimistic objectivity, counselling ability, general luck with others as long as there are no deep commitments, philosophies differ in the relationship, gains support from parent-in-law, overweight or underweight spouse, when applicable, strong similarities in first and second marriage, children and spouse create mutual clashes, financial luck through marriage and partnership, financial losses through broken relationships, legal conflicts with family, very small family.

Retrograde Jupiter Through the Eighth House. Luck through combined values/assets, strong mystical interest and occult philosophies, corporate connections or involvement, strong personal influence used to get to places in life, strategies with faith, hidden luck when needed, inheritance, tax benefits, sexual idealism or taking the fulfillment for granted, blind ambition, justified philosophies, prays for good luck, secret religious involvements, death of beliefs and reborn idealism, grand exits, spouse controls the resources, personal philosophies compromised towards mass beliefs, strict upbringing.

Retrograde Jupiter Through the Ninth House. Philosophically oriented and stuck with beliefs, faith overtakes a lot of other life areas, idealism to the extreme that forces eventual compromise, lucky second marriage despite diverse mutual philosophies, delays or blocks in higher education, fears of legal battles or phobias toward litigation, complex stresses through children and marriage, total change of life beliefs in mid-life period, self-prophecies do not work, driven by blind faith, recognition and publicity needed, self-conscious, low opinions regarding institutions, travel and escapement fantasies.

Retrograde Jupiter Through the Tenth House. Ambitious, ego conscious, and goal oriented, philosophically driven career, strong pride in one's faith, clash with superiors on tactical matters, government, bureaucracy or chain of commands important. Major key changes in career directions in mid life, ambition curbs all of a sudden, willing to accept blame and responsibility, competes with father and even excels him in life, purpose of direction highly crucial. Career given substantial priority over family/home, diplomatic but authoritative, administers well, takes charge under pressure, least threatened by circumstances.

Retrograde Jupiter Through the Eleventh House. Large group associations, great feel for friends, comprehends other's problems, friendships on an idealistic basis, luck through friendly contacts. Authority displayed in friendships, willing to compromise beliefs to secure friendships. Expects a lot of freedom and independence from others. Offsprings cause sudden concerns and problems, reborn attitudes in second half of life, optimistic about the life goals, hopeful till the end, indulges in group meditation.

Retrograde Jupiter Through the Twelfth House. Strong sense of spiritual destiny and mystical magnetism, very evolved soul in terms of Karmic achievements. This life as a coffee-break to observe others with adequate interference, luck behind-the-scene, follows the leader, once faith is established, psychic/perceptive dreams, deals isolation calmly and cooly, unlocks universal secrets, fear of mistakes, sorrows from involvements, quite esoteric and spiritual growth in last years of life. Slow disappearance from life, gets high on worldly events and God's creation, hospitals/institutional contacts. Disperses his teaching to others on a limited basis, inner psychological complexes.

RETROGRADE JUPITER RULING THE HOUSES

Retrograde Jupiter Ruling the First House. Personal ambition gets curtailed due to circumstances around him. In early life, he would want to climb the mountain of success. However, as the time goes on, he realizes his true place in life, which curbs his previously planned goals. often security and peace are found within him and not out somewhere else in the crowd. His faith in himself dwindles, but the uncertainties are actually his tools of self awareness. Metaphysical, occult interests descent upon him all of a sudden as the universal coincidences make sense to him. Self conscious, freedom loving, and independence nature seen here. However, within himself he knows his master's voice. Optimistic nature requires control as he gets sudden responsibility in life. Once he overcomes that, he can free himself for a while. Goals are important to this native, but he changes them frequently. His beliefs and philosophies often do not work for him but they can be excellent to others. As a result, his teachings may be followed by others around him. Body weight fluctuates here along with the achievable personal luck factor. Thus, under indulgive happy period, he gains volume and can lose it when adverse situations surround him. Far away people come into his life abruptly, emphasizing the Karmic achievements from interfering with the current and future situations.

Retrograde Jupiter Ruling the Second House. Financial fluctuations or major changes in them are quite likely here. Philosophical values undergo a major turn around, showing his faith and belief, roller coaster of life. Ambition to collect and accumulate worth can be strong. However, once he achieves that, he goes after different universal values. A sense of spirituality is associated with his resources. Thus, donations, charities, or give-aways can be important to him, in the hope of better Karma in future life times. He is willing to publicize his worth as long as it helps him gain some more of it. Deep down, he wants to be secretive, self sufficient and immune to circumstances. He may not like financial responsibility as he equates money and pleasure together, rather than money and authoritative status. Learning experiences through financial, institutional, and legalities are seen. However, he does tumble on the same curve again and again. Benefits through family often occur and there is a strong woman's influence behind this native for financial achievements. He can be possessive of others, but at the same time he requires freedom in partnership. In his financial optimism, he may not worry about money matters, as things just come to him when needed in adequate fashion. Goals are more important to him than the means to achieve them.

Retrograde Jupiter Ruling the Third House. Exaggerations or over optimistic attitudes are displayed by the native. Mental confidence is shown without proper beliefs behind it to support the strength by him. Taking chances on a mental level or promising something that cannot be fulfilled. As a result, the native becomes acutely unreliable. A large family seen here that includes many brothers and sisters. If not, the native will have a large circle of people around him with similar type or relationships. Travel can be very important and the native is optimistic about the opportunities. He shows good promise and intelligence in early education but may bluff his way out in higher education and learnings. His ideas, communications and advice has substantial generosity behind it, as the native can be quite lucky regarding the mental resources. His mannerism can be polite, authoritative, and humorously serious. Thinking on a large scale or planning an elaborate strategy can be significant here. Philosophies tend to be logical but his approach in using them may not be very logical or methodical. Domestic discipline, family stability, and general standards can be strict. However, all the children usually stick together to combat the parents.

Retrograde Jupiter Ruling the Fourth House. Domestic philosophies may be much too flexible, ideological, and ill-defined for the native to follow through. As a result, he differs with family tradition and domestic rules and regulations. He may get a lot of freedom and independence in his early childhood, but he desires the opposite. As a result of this excessive freedom, weaker family ties can be possible. Contacts with people much older than him or grandparental connections play significant role in his growth. Benefits through family inheritance, real estate, property, land, etc., can be important. He likes and enjoys large home structures or free spaces. Quite independence seeking mother seen here or her life can be uniquely defined. Her philosophical, metaphysical, and religious inheritance is received by the native and later in future strong spiritual communication may continue. Domestic responsibility may often be neglected by the native, giving his spouse a greater burden or share of it. He enjoys casual entertaining at home and groups often converge on key philosophical tune. Father-in-law can be prominent and well-to-do in the society in many cases. Life security, stability, and good foundation is important to him but he is not willing to put efforts to achieve that. He hopes for the best and often gets close to his expectations in life.

Retrograde Jupiter Ruling the Fifth House. Quite casual attitude displayed in love/romance in this case. The native wants independence but coexistance in the interaction. Romanticism can be very spontaneous and emotionally uplifting for this native but he prefers 'no strings attached' type of policy. Philosophies and standards differ in the inter-personal relationship but the native can be very optimistic about the outcome. He takes chances that might sound unreasonable to others. Speculative luck is very unpredictable but provides sensation to this native. Idealism and goals can be very significant in the romantic exchange compared to the participating efforts. A lot of freedom given to the children or the native can be free from serious responsibility from the offsprings. He is independently creative and individualistic in the achievements. Outdoor sports, physical activities, and dynamic gambling tendencies are significant. The person enjoys long term goal and creative fantasies of life, but he is not too keen on filling the intermediate details. The casual attitude shown in romance often instigates others to fall in love with this native. Very small family or even lack of children likely here. In life, he may start off with nothing in terms of financial worth, but he will achieve good success. However, it is hard for him to maintain that success soon after he achieves it.

Retrograde Jupiter Ruling the Sixth House. Considerable fluctuations, changes and slow growth in work and services areas are noticed. Here the native wants freedom and independence on the job that his superiors may not be willing to give him. As a result, a clash of values, philosophies, and standards occur on the job. He wants to do things his own way and cannot really stand hindrance from others. His services can be philosophically, administratively and managerially oriented. He knows how to supervise and get the job done through proper coordination. However, his immediate boss does not feel his methods are capable in achieving the objectives. Financial compensation associated with work may seem inadequate, tempting him to look for greener pastures elsewhere. He might be allergic to grass, pollen, vegetation, or outdoors. However, love of the water and aquatics can be important here. Problems with fluid retention, enlargement of the liver, or muscle tensions are likely in this case. In spite of changes in jobs, he often gets lucky in locating another one. Good luck or proper contacts from mother's side of the family helps the native periodically. He often takes a big bite out of work share, but he may not finish all he initiates. Over optimism on the job needs control and periodic curbing by him.

Retrograde Jupiter Ruling the Seventh House. More than one marriage or attitude towards the interactions are very free and independence seeking. The native has a phobia of confinement in the secure relationship. As a result, he may always have an escape route to get out of it, just in case he feels like it. Often the spouse can be very freedom loving, forcing the native to accept that in the situation. Here open, blunt, and optimistic attitude prevails in the relationship even though both parties may not agree upon it. Sarcastic objectivity or philosophical reversals often noticed in him. Socializing can be an integral part of this personality, but it has to be free-floating and free of pressures. Gypsy attitude towards life may be noticed. Instead of compromising in marriage the native may abandon it or his spouse does the same. Quite objective philosophies seen here, but others are convinced of their realism eventually. In many cases, the native may remain a bachelor in order to pursue his own life style. Inheritance potential or luck through grandparents is significant and probable here. He may have a lot of open enemies but their philosophies stimulate him considerably in various areas of life. He likes to take things for granted; but when they do not occur as expected, he just moves on to something different.

Retrograde Jupiter Ruling the Eighth House. Excellent spiritual and metaphysical awareness or interest seen here. Luck through combined resources can be possible, if he can manage to stick with his patience. Happy-go-lucky attitude towards sexuality noticed. However, he takes mutual fulfillment for granted. In doing so, he may appear insensitive to the physical needs of his spouse. Sexuality is looked upon something very spiritual and the common blend of beliefs triggers his physical passions. Sexual control or discipline may not be easily achieved here without the curtain of philosophy and spirituality. Inheritance potential can be significant but last minute reversals could be expected. Corporate finances, banking, institutional management, credit control, psychological counselling, medicine, or surgery, etc., can be significant in his professional area. Interest in reincarnation, life after death, or rebirth of one's consciousness can be important in his life. Major events, boosts, or upward growth occurs in his life after separation or passing away of someone around him. He can be very optimistic about this credit spending, creating financial drain unexpectedly. Freedom from combined assets is needed and expected by him, but he is not that lucky in its fulfillment. As a result, his spouse may outsmart his possessive attitude regarding financial manipulation control.

Retrograde Jupiter Ruling the Ninth House. Excellent philosophical and metaphysical achievements seen here. The native is free to pursue his path in the spiritual directions without earthy hindrance from others. His own philosophies are of great value to him or they guide him as long as he maintains faith in them. Always in search of the universal understanding, he is willing to learn and relearn the same thing if he has to. This perpetual studentship helps him perfect in this life. Idealogy and golden goals are very crucial here. The optimism and prudence shown by him can be followed by many afterwards. Good success in at least part of his life will be noticed. Dealing with different standards, cultures, beliefs, or philosophies seen in his interpersonal relationships. Actually, he is born and raised in a very philosophically conscious environment. Religion or institutional discipline can be important in his life. When applicable the second marriage will be very individualized personal coexistance. Freedom and uniqueness often demanded in it or noticed without choice. Exceptional third child or that child may not contribute to continued family expansion. Travel, relocations, distant environments, etc., can be significant in his life. Higher learning, administrative management, legalities, and good institutional connections are significant, but minor delays in education seen.

Retrograde Jupiter Ruling the Tenth House. Quite good career success and expansion of opportunities seen. The native may not be fully satisfied with one sense of achievement. As a result, he may change his career or profession all of a sudden and achieve success in the new direction as well. Power, will, and the willpower all blend easily here forming a stronger personality. Clash with father or beliefs differ with him in this case. Constant competition to outdo his own father and any of his life long ideas are seen here. His idealism works nicely for success and achievements outside the home. Domestic areas may not be very successful or his own interest in it can be dwindling periodically. Administrative, management, or political success seen associated with career. He may have to swallow his pride and ego on the job. However, he allows that to happen so that he can "get-even" with others later on. Under pressure, he prefers to be alone, independent and isolated. Sarcasm and controlled optimism comes out under those situations. Strong support from in-laws might be seen here. In politics or high-level responsibility, he has to be careful of his own convictions as they can backfire upon him bringing significant downfall in life.

Retrograde Jupiter Ruling the Eleventh House. Friendships and group associations are often selected based upon the common beliefs and philosophies. However, in this case the native realizes the common grounds are not what he expects them to be for continued friendship. Subsequently, his interest is lost in the interaction and he withdraws away slowly from it. He starts off with high goals and idealogy regarding his hopes of life. However, soon he realizes his over-estimation, damping his efforts of achievements to a lower gear. Freedom and independence are expected from his close friendships, but somehow he does not get that. Mystical, philosophical, and religious orientation can be significant in that interaction. However, financial and material intervention disrupts the relation periodically. Mutual values create ego manipulations and both parties drift apart. Financial betterment can often be seen through his friendships as he learns different techniques and strategies of life achievements. Love received can be quite fluctuating for him. Thus, when he says leave me alone, others do that easily. However, he really does not mean isolation from them, but just non-interference. Subsequently, he feels hurt and unloved through his own actions. Financial benefits through his father's side are important and he encounters with sickness from his mother's side.

Retrograde Jupiter Ruling the Twelfth House. A strong sense of Karmic and spiritual awareness seen here. The native is willing to sacrifice in this life with a faith that it goes on his account for the future life. Outwardly, he may be cautious, conservative, and practical. For some reason, he cannot continue his spiritual mission in this life which he started in the recent past incarnation. The coffee-break taken in this life for material purposes is fully justified by all universal authorities. Security and structure are highly needed for him in this life as those things hold him down to earth. Without these holding forces, his spirit is much too independence seeking to live on earth. Hidden concern for financial matters seen here but he gets what he needs at the last minute. Strong but deep subconscious can be felt here with power of the will working behind him. Maturity occurs within him quite early in life as he can count upon his past life wisdom and philosophies to his assistance. When left alone, day dreams and fantasies take over his personality. As a result, he will often keep himself busy and occupied. At the middle part in life, he will completely open up and greatly expose his hangups in order to better understand his personality. Politics, strategies and complex friendships noticed here in association with his career. Health problems, weight gains/losses, liver complaints or muscular disorder may be noticed in later years of life.

RETROGRADE JUPITER OPPOSITE MOON

A key woman's influence is very substantial in the life of this native. Mixed situations occur in the interaction and the native learns substantial lessons from her. Her assistance as well as periodic interference cause sudden reversals in the mutual needs. Life beliefs and philosophies are compromised in order to get emotional satisfaction, security, and sympathy. Mother-figure is very important in life with or without the actual mother. Here anyone who provides the emotional exchanges, nurturing, and pampering is automatically bestowed that title unconsciously. Home and domestic foundation take over any other achievements from the outside world. Education that is not directly used to secure a better life stability is certainly neglected. He wants to be popular, confident and self-satisfied at home. For that reason, he adjusts his life philosophies accordingly. Home gains the priority over distant travel, far away places, and relatives. Thus, the native may indulge better in the backyard picnic than go on the exciting safari. People of different background, culture, and heritage unconsciously threaten him, bringing his suppressed racism out slightly. Those things may create complex learning experiences in his life. Unexpected or long drawn legal battles with a woman are quite likely here. Great respect for mother seen here and the native may follow her philosophies, values and standards quite blindly. In a man's chart, this indicates mother figure replacement in his spouse or spouse will be competing with his mother's image in life. In a woman's case, it may indicate some sudden conflicting issues with woman associated with her institutional matters. Here she has to get involved with larger groups and institutions where women are the majority. The native does not like to exaggerate but in his own emotional feeling areas he is often compelled to do so. He will take all chances and be optimistic towards a happy and blissful home status. Benefits through home, property and real estate are quite possible and more significantly from the mother's side of the family. Emotions and imagination are given strong priority over the philosophical/mystical jargon. He wants a life real, simple, but enjoyable at home without counting upon the esoteric, spiritual, or mystical phenomenon. Thus, he may not care what happens in the world or universe as long as he is content at home.

RETROGRADE JUPITER OPPOSITE SUN

Considerable drive, power, or ambition is noticed here. Success in life is not easy, as the native has to swallow his pride on various curbs. Compromised beliefs and philosophies are visible no matter what he goes after to achieve in life. Higher education is often sacrificed as he feels content in his basic lower education. Thus, he will find no special need to be highly educated in life. If by some chance he educates to that level, he may not truly use it for the best direct advantage in life. There is always some financial activity or scheme going on in his mind. Money, values and resources are important here as considerable changes occur in his financial status in life. He respects and abides by his father and he can look up to him as an ideal person. He will adapt and follow whatever the philosophical ethical, and moral stand his father has in life. At times this following can be totally blindly done. A respect for authority and superiority is created from within, as he knows he will be in that spot when others will respect him as well. In love-romance, he will compromise his beliefs, standards, and philosophies as he can be intensely attracted to such situations. Taking chances in love-romance or even towards his offsprings are significant. He is willing to get down on his knees if he has to to achieve the objective in the relationship. Strong pride is visible otherwise. Creativity is very substantial here so are his calculated risks in life. To boost his image, the native will exaggerate without hesitation. In a woman's chart, father figure replacement is noticed in her search for a spouse. It could be the early void in her life from father in a real or psychological sense. In a political situation, uncommon publicity is achieved, but he can fall off the great image suddenly and unexpectedly. The public issues and his sympathy towards others will put him in a lime light. However, the lime light can turn into miserable sunburn from the public criticism of his flexible philosophies. In many cases, multiple marriages or complex issues involving second marriages and the children from the first marriage are seen. Major changes usually occur in his life time in the middle age and he makes substantial transition in the life values, beliefs, and philosophies here.

RETROGRADE JUPITER OPPOSITE MERCURY

Great tensions between logic and philosophies noticed here with logic taking the winning punch. Philosophies, beliefs, and standards are compromised in various ways of life so that the native can maintain the logical track. Exaggerations, over estimation, and excessive thinking seen. Strain in the brain caused by inner indecisions within affects the native in terms of nervous excess. Many efforts often converge behind the scene or just help him on an inner psychological level as the times goes on, or he unfolds himself very well along the spiritual path. Faith is often substantial within him towards any achievement, but he has to compromise that in the light of earthy practicality. Means over-ride the goals in this case. Thus, the native prefers how he can handle the opportunity rather than what it can be. Communication, learning, expression, and counselling can be an integral part of majority of his life efforts and purposes. Brother/sisters, and closer family environment are always given much higher priority compared to distant relatives. Education is important for him, but he may not indulge in higher learnings. Connections associated with distant countries, foreign people, cultures, legalities, and institutional matters seen here but with periodic complex dealings. Neighborhood associations are important here without agreeing to their cause. He is an excellent logical communicator and able to teach with methodology. He does not believe in what he does, he can simply justify it using reasoning. Synthesis, diagnosis, and analysis are very important to this native, rather than the principle, goal, expectations, or meanings. He wants to achieve success on a lower, earthy plane first. For that reason, he may even compromise his esoteric worth or willing to give up his position in the line of spirituality. This down to earth preference helps him fulfill a lot of Karma in this life. Short travel, nearby trips are considerably significant than frequent long journeys. Simple mannerism attracts him more than the social display of grace and charm.

RETROGRADE JUPITER OPPOSITE VENUS

Indulgent, extravagant, but enriched personality seen here. Things are often done with enthusiasm and excess of feelings. Beliefs and philosophies are often compromised to keep better harmony in marriage and personal life. Money, values, and resources are much more significant to the native than any standards, ethics or conventionality. Thus, the goal in life is to achieve things that would pleasurize him on a material level. Esoteric, philosophical or spiritual substitutes are not readily accepted by him instead of real worldly pleasure. A thing of beauty is joy forever for him. Femininity, delicacy, emotionalism, feelings, artistic beauty, pleasurable display, etc., are very important here. Over indulgence in good things is contagious and habit forming can be very easily seen here. He does not like to take chances and at times he can be a parasite to somebody's good luck. Calm, ease, comfort, and take the middle road attitude seen. Emotional over expansion, self-consciousness, and great value orientation seen in the relationship. Social involvement and social activities are must for him. Family cohesion is noticed but on a smaller scale. Thus, he may neglect the family he comes from and put considerably more focus upon his spouse and kids. Traditions and family heritage may be compromised in order to enjoy his own relationship. He establishes his own standards, ethics, and morality in the light of his spouse and he is well driven by them in life. Unusual publicity is associated with this individual. Thus, he may be known for certain facets of life in one portion of the society. Adaptability is seen here associated with versatility. Thus, the native may not challenge and oppose others but will get what he wants through uncommon means. Feelings are more predominant than his sexual, sensational, type of indulgence. Contacts and associations play a key role in his socializing. Thus, he knows where and how he should mix with others in the society.

RETROGRADE JUPITER OPPOSITE MARS

Speculative tendencies, risk taking, and chancy attitude seen here. Actions dominate the calculated risk, coupled with luck, creating unpredictable outcomes. Impatience becomes the worst enemy as the last minute action may not be consistent with the prior planning. Substantial financial activities, fluctuations in resources and token gambling tendencies are seen. The native is much too active to just sit tight and not do anything in life. As a result, he indulges in taking chances and dabbles in speculation. Even the most practical people under this combination have difficulty being just conservative. Optimism, luck, and prudence are there, but the native relies greatly upon his energies, actions, and zest. The dynamic personality forces his foresight to take a day off as he enjoys the sensation of risks and chances. Anything that comes in easy is not pleasurable to this native. Values, efforts, and investment terminology are applied here in various areas of life. Philosophies, standards, and morality may be compromised to fit the individual needs. Self comes first, then the social values is the philosophy visible here. There is a feeling of great superiority over others of different background and culture. Thus, a glimpse of racism, hypocracy, and excessive self-pride are likely. He believes in himself and the force behind him. For that reason, he may even neglect legalities, moralities, and social justice. 'Being up and above law' attitude needs control. Athletic interests, sporting spirit, and excellent game plan are a part of this native. Competitive spirit helps him get to places others may not even dream of. Life can be full of hurdles and challenges to this native, which he joyfully accepts. Some complex relationships with children or regarding them likely. Muscles, blood, and tissues are key focal areas which require periodic attention. Either good or bad extremes are possible in that respect. Religious rebellion may be noticed here and the native may become more superior than the social supremacy. In a woman's chart, it often indicates powerful spouse with much different mutual philosophies. Her standards are partially compromised for better self-fulfillment in life. Families often hinder or they are sacrificed to achieve individual success.

RETROGRADE JUPITER OPPOSITE SATURN

The struggle between conservative and liberal sides of the personality noticed here with the conservative side winning at the end. A lot of such conflict is stirred within, expanded but practically used for constructive purposes. Family and traditions are given ultimate superiority over one's enlarged philosophies. Beliefs and optimism are consumed within to produce a better structure for outward display. Morality and ethics might appear very strong and at times morbid to the limit, but the native is compelled in that direction unconsciously. The native may not want to take any chances or risks even though calculated luck might be with him. He may go for slow but steady chance to achieve things in life, rather than out manipulate the odds of universality. Rigidity and solid structure are very important foundations of his goals. He would rather under-estimate than fall short of his estimation. Pessimism might be seen in this native almost by virtue of inheritance. Stick in the mud attitude, displaying cold shoulder or getting periodic cold feet are most likely in this combination. Legalities create complex events in his life as he changes his attitudes suddenly and decides to go straight. Problems in higher education are noticed which may affect his professional accomplishments. A sense of pride, duty, and respect is very impressive in this case that can show honesty, straight forwardness, and country appeal. Going by the book is important here compared to any inspired idealogy. Goals are very selective, practical and achievable. Strong family background, rigid orientation, and support seen behind him. He respects the authority rather than the philosophy behind it. Thus, his loyalty is with the person and not the reason behind that person. Long and deep friendships are seen here with special preserving ingredient. He can show excellent patience under pressure. As a matter of fact, he performs better when a lot of circumstances crowd him. Slow but steady success in the career seen and he just has to achieve that in spite of much politics behind-the-scene against him. He can easily become the victim of other's ambition, but then he just gets up and trots on ahead with equal enthusiasm.

RETROGRADE JUPITER OPPOSITE URANUS

Philosophies and beliefs are often compromised to please the friendships. Group associations become very important in his life compared to his basic standards and concepts set forth by his family. Educational pursuits may be compromised in order to better serve his life goals. Unusuality and unconventionality gain the upper hand in his basic life make-up. Learning and relearning experiences from legalities, second marriage, hound him. Eventually, his friendships become the relief point for him. Luck is counted upon by him, but it can be very delicate and uncertain as to the outcome. Thus, it is best he takes no chances in pursuing his goals. Institutional compromise of his philosophies make him the odd ball in the group. However, they all admire him for his unique stand on the issues. Religious rebellion is often seen here and the native may go totally against his basic life concepts and understandings. A sense of spirituality is modified by virtue of universal uniqueness. Thus, in the process of achieving the uncommon status one has to swallow his pride at certain steps of the way. Calculated risks or unique plans become the unlocking key to his goals rather than assumed good luck. Optimism may be kept low as he realizes the good fortune may not be with him. Religion, metaphysics, administration, and institutions of uncommon nature are significant here. As much as he is unique and different from others, racism may be mildly embedded in him. He is fighting for his unique/uncommon identity at the same time going by double standards. Perceptions and wisdom can be present here but his search is more important to be a virtue of path rather than the actual goal. He may be after the same universal truth others are looking for. However, he pleasurizes during his search and the challenge is important to him. Considerable family adaptations might be done in his life due to sudden circumstances. He would rather invent a new thing than indulge in the kingly luxury given to him by somebody. Thus, self-created kicks are enjoyable to him more than any spoon-fed sensation.

RETROGRADE JUPITER OPPOSITE NEPTUNE

Excellent exposure in the area of spirituality, and esoteric interests are noticed here. The native may fluctuate from his life beliefs, background, and culture to get into something that has more universal appeal. Creative expression and indulgive fantasies can be very important here. Getting into the areas of institutions, hospitals, or service industries can be of significance. Relatives often differ with him in terms of life goals, stands, or living arrangements. A sense of hidden appeal towards the unknown seen here. The native may sacrifice a standard, normal road to go into risky path. Behind-the-scene events have considerable impact upon the native. He can be imaginative, perceptive and unrealistic when it comes to producing creative output. Self is often consumed within, as the fantasies and the unreality provide him good sensation in the areas of his choice. Legalities and institutional matters get in the way of his life success. Thus, conflicts through his own counsel or the legal misadvise possible in this case. Need to runaway and escape from his family tradition, beliefs, and philosophies seen. At times, it is the family structure that drives him to do so. Nursing, medicine, pharmacies, or dealing with patient/services area in focus here. Excellent healing or mediumistic talent is visible. Constant inner expansion or explosion gives rise to creative display. This periodic outburst of creativity can be constructively used towards something very imaginative and productive. Ultra creative goals need extra attention here as the native may over-shoot his limits. Lessons to be learned regarding optimism or overly enthusiastic expectations have a tendency to repeat periodically. Complex attitudes, mild racism, cultural resentments are all feasible here and working well behind-the-scenes. The native projects one image outwardly but inside his heart may say another regarding others in his life. Fantasized trips, far away escapism, and imaginative indulgence are significant in the unconscious domain. He can be psycho-sensitive. His reactions to others' probling of his subconscious are very unpredictable and rejective type.

RETROGRADE JUPITER OPPOSITE PLUTO

A sense of inner being is often challenged due to circumstances. Occult philosophies are emphasized here and native has to swallow his pride in getting into something new. Standards, concepts, and beliefs of life are modified and restructured completely. Good psychological understanding, metaphysical awareness and a sense of deep penetration noticed. He is willing to do things that have far more deeper significance than just on the surface type. Dealing with others' resources or converting their life values seen in terms of some key universalization. Mystery attracts him and he accepts challenge quickly at the cost of detaching from his philosophical foundation. Institutional matters are important to him as he considers their foundation a holy base. Strategy becomes the goal with optimism a secondary criteria in its achievement. Family compromise might be done to enlighten one's life from within. Combined resources can be the frontier for achieving the common philosophies. Higher education may be compromised in order to build better family finances. Thus, the native may have responsibilities upon his shoulder early in life, making him sacrifice his educational needs. Once he fulfills his family obligations, he is free to pursue his educational and philosophical interests later in life. Second marriage becomes highlighted in this case, and whenever applicable. In areas dealing with taxes, credit, insurance, psychological-occult counselling, the native may deteriorate his standards to fit the simple practical demands of the profession. Good detective tendencies, ability to penetrate others and excellent philosophical combat are noticed. Problems away from the birth place are seen or events occur with involvements from people of different culture and backgrounds. The pride and optimism should be kept adaptable in this case, as the native walks through life with many compromising situations. Benefits through insurance matters and legalities seen. Litigations can be a key area in life that needs attention. He can combat legalities much better than initiate such actions. Thus, it is best he does not start any legal proceedings towards the spouse or other partnerships.

RETROGRADE SATURN

The retrogradation of Saturn creates an awareness of self limitation. The native identifies inner phobias, insecurities, and individual liabilities. However, he has strong self-protective and self-preserving instincts. Life does not always start rosey for him or he feel he is in a wrong family. Family difficulties, coping with the tradition and authority make him feel inferior. As a result, inferiority complex gathers within. Building a protective cover for his circumstantial hurt relieves stresses for a while. However, he has to prove himself out in the world, for his own sake. Here the over compensation of self-assertiveness is noticed to justify one's own ego. This duality of personality can make him very timid at times, but he has the capability to be a roaring lion. He respects an authority, even though he resents the person behind it in the hope of being an authority someday in the future. Problems with father are visible. Either he has to compete with him viciously or he tries very hard to be totally different from him. In a woman's chart, domineering father forces her to be thick-skinned but quite mellow inside. However, in many cases, she replaces him with a husband that is just like father. Down falls and intense recovery in professional goals seen. The native has to work hard to achieve his objectives but at the same time his ascent to the top is very complex. Fears, phobias, superstitious tendencies and pessimism are closely associated here. The native can be very introverted and spend significant time of his life in isolation, seculsion, or in making a comeback strategy. Persistent stubbornness is noticed, but his authority and ruling over others are not long lasting. Blaming the circumstances, complaining of the injustice and hiding under the non-existent luck can be seen here. Substantial learning lessons in life noticed here and the second third of life can be the most active period in his achievements. Dealing with family responsibility and making sure you do not unload something similar to your offspring is noticed here. Due to circumstances and often from his own doing, he feels humiliated by others. This may all be in his own mind as most of this ill-fated humility comes from his self-punishing attitude. Masochism and frustrations from over-estimations are seen. A sense of security, stability, and foundation is very important to him but he has a hard time maintaining that in life.

RETROGRADE SATURN THROUGH THE HOUSES

Retrograde Saturn Through the First House. Self-limiting, misunderstood self image, conservative, practical, mature and deals with people of different ages, projects discontinuous confidence, patient when not needed, concern for older people and old age, circumstantially controlled, accident prone or clumsiness, near sighted, efforts more important than the goals, mild masochism, weak health and confining events in early life. Compromises in partnerships.

Retrograde Saturn Through the Second House. Financial concerns, material reserves, projects poverty when rich and vice versa, gains and losses through older people, learns through money and values. Frozen assets, controlled optimism, financial inferiorities, hung-up on values, ends justify the means, loyalty expected in marriage and interactions, security transforms to confinement. Difficulty pleasing the family in spite of values and worth, mid-life crisis hits him hard, stingy at time due to forced circumstances, subdued voice pattern and speech.

Retrograde Saturn Through the Third House. Mental disorientation or self-discipline backfires, morbid thinking, detachments from brother/sisters with or without self choice. Weak audio response, pessimistic communication, delays in travel or phobias in motion. Health problems to father, sexual withdrawals due to serious mentality, a loner or prefers isolation, hidden stresses to mother, mental discipline in normal dosage brings good attitudes and achievements, slow learning process or learns through mistakes of his or others, sense of purpose and life goals important.

Retrograde Saturn Through the Fourth House. Domestic problems or feeling of home-confinements, older folks at home, cannot stand living in the family but difficulty in getting out of it. Family responsibility falls heavy upon him. Roots and traditions are hard to get away from, depressions through mother. Benefits through property, real-estate or land. However, a lot of delays and anxiety associated with family inheritance expected. Family guardianship, spirits at home, root significance important. Difficulty in childhood, self-punishing attitudes and emotional compromises.

Retrograde Saturn Through the Fifth House. Delays, difficulties and frustrations in love romance, children create concern or problems with birth likely, cautious and conservative attitude in personal emotional expressions, frigidity likely, romantic depressions, speculative delays or losses, serious attitude towards lower education, morbid ideas regarding pleasurism, domestic problems around mid-life, financial inadequacies from mother's side of the family, gardening, agriculture, pottery or practical arts, patience and persistance shown in personal life expectations.

Retrograde Saturn Through the Sixth House. Weak health or acute problems surface periodically, teeth, bones, skin infections, arthritic conditions, colds and allergies are likely. Hard working conditions, learning lessons and confinements through own health or someone else's around him. Longevity in the family from the mother's side, manipulative hindrance from the relatives, especially due to hidden events from spouse's family. Patience is a virtue on the job but others walk over him and take advantage of it, swallowed pride, inferiorities or insecurities due to co-workers, abrupt changes in jobs and health status.

Retrograde Saturn Through the Seventh House. Practical and material orientation towards marriage, pessimistic objectivity, people do not come up to their expectations, swallowing of harsh reality, patience shown towards others but dissatisfactions in spite of it, rigid rules, regulations and discipline binds the relationship to a point of suffocations. Cannot live with and without marriage, creating immunity towards it. Age or maturity level difference needed in the interaction, late marriage seen. More than one marriage only under stressful circumstances, antisocial or self discipline detaches from others, gets high on feeling sorry for others, demands strict standards.

Retrograde Saturn Through the Eighth House. Controlled physical drive, neutrality or damping on sexual energies. Sex as a subserving tool, disciplined passions with or without choice, morbid sexual fantasies and subsequent fears and phobias. Inhibitions closely associated with tradition and upbringing. Feels guilty and low towards excessive use of physical passion. Problems with combined resources or marries someone less lucky than him. Occult skepticism, delays in credit and taxes due to stick-in-the-mud attitude, distorted psychological profile, long life but fears of death due to confinements. Close observations of death.

Retrograde Saturn Through the Ninth House. Strong religious beliefs implanted but resents his own kind. Life standards are looked upon as liabilities, transition from prejudice to antiprejudice, delays in higher education or nonapplications of education to practical usage, fear of travel and long journey, anti-institutional, distorted sense of justice with dual beliefs. Problems in second marriage or its true existance. Hidden fears or difficulties to father, lack of recognition and formal success, believes in materialism but it does not believe in the native.

Retrograde Saturn Through the Tenth House. Tries very hard in career, willing to grind his nose for success, difficulty pleasing the father, lack of approval and acceptance through the parent, pessimistic under pressure. Superiors with big age or generational difference, stiff ego with perpetual persistance, respects authority in the hope of being an authority someday. A lot of skepticism but inwardly believes in fate. Ambition curbs down by mid-life period, but comes up surging later in life. Hard working father or lack of luck to him, practical profession pursued.

Retrograde Saturn Through the Eleventh House. Friends with age and maturity differences, lacks recognition from others, dry social life, withdraws easily from others, lack of love received through friends as his cold behavior obstructs the flow. Mild morbidity in the goals and hopes of life. Inner fights between conservative and nonconservative attitudes, unique cautions, unusual conventionality, selective of friends, seldom indulges in frequent group participations. Major career changes in the middle-third part of life. Liabilities through offsprings.

Retrograde Saturn Through the Twelfth House. Hidden problems, fights a losing battle with circumstances, phobias and fears carried through past life, very difficult previous incarnation and the current life shows partial tinge of it, confinements seen due to his own choice of circumstances, self created liabilities. Karmic pay-off, insomnia, works hard behind-the-scene. Others steal the credit of his efforts. Success in late years of life. Mature identity is displayed since childhood, optimism imagined but pessimism worshiped. Skepticism towards mysticism and spirituality but eventually he becomes a thorough believer.

RETROGRADE SATURN RULING THE HOUSES

Retrograde Saturn Ruling the First House. Personal insecurities, inferiorities or loss of self-confidence seen here. The native has to work hard for his rewards. He strongly believes in destiny, luck and fate due to events and circumstances in his life. The native may have a gloomy and pessimistic attitude along with self repressive tendencies. Although he has patience and stamina to do things till their completion, his negative attitude often holds him back to intiate several situations. Being a rigid wet blanket, he casts a pessimistic shadow over his own surrounding support. A sense of overly mature nature, untimely aging or just pretending to be old and fragile personality likely in this case. One's own obstinacy and personal doubts about self achievements can be the worst enemy in this case. Dealing with repeated responsibility, unfair and unjustified pressure and circumstantial confinements noticed here. He can achieve wonders with his stamina, patience, persistance, and controlled optimism, once he understands himself and overcomes his own impedences. Life security becomes his confinement and often it appears he is asking for punishment for his own reasons. Excellent practical, material outlook seen here, but he may not be financially successful.

Retrograde Saturn Ruling the Second House. Financial cautiousness is often forced upon the native and he has to learn substantial lessons through resources or by lack of it. Material orientations associated with financial limitations noticed here. Life values fluctuate and he tries hard to run away from family tradition. When he wants resources, they become scarce and finally when he gives-up that pursuit, things happen very easy fo him. As a persistent and patient slave of circumstances, material world creates inferiorities and pessimism to him. He has to work hard to achieve his resources and values. In this situation, money does not multiply and grow without efforts. Family responsibility, burdon, and unnecessary frustrations created in life. Although he may appear rugged, harsh, and strong in character, his insides are very vulnerable, touchy, and emotionally sensitive. He will cry poor when he has some resources left. However, when poor, he will behave exactly opposite. Unusual thinking, ideas, and planning noticed in his mental achievements. Strong work-career orientation is forced upon him bringing his ego out that will adapt with the surroundings. He can save resources very well, but his emotional mistakes cost him financial strain. Outward aggressive masculinity may be seen inspite of inner femininity that demands attentions from others. Defective right side of the body, bone, joints, right eye or right shoulder possible.

Retrograde Saturn Ruling the Third House. Mind, mentality and thinking process are affected here due to retrogradation. Inhibited thinking or lack of confidence in one's own ideas are seen as the native vacillates on mental level. Mental discipline or practical seriousness actually works against the native. Difficulties with older brothers/sisters likely as the native feels much below·their levels in life achievements. A pessimistic, melancholy and to the point communication noticed here. Delays and anxiety in the lower education or with formal logic seen in this case. Somehow, the native has to grow in the company of people with great age difference creating inferiority. Mental strategies backfire or he acts much later than expected causing frustrations. Unusual and withdrawn mannerism noticed and periodic mental depressions possible. The native works hard to achieve mental security or projects stable mentality. Communicative problems on the job or with superiors seen. Deficient hearing or unconsciously not paying attention to what others say is noticed. Misunderstandings, improper interpretations. or taking things for granted occur here. A rebellious unreliability shown by him, but he is very sensitive to any criticism of his beliefs. He is sensitive to surrounding environmental depressions or wrong environments depress him quickly.

Retrograde Saturn Ruling the Fourth House. The native cannot stand the family, heritage, and domestic issues. However, he has difficulty running away from it all. Not able to detach himself from what he does not really care for, makes him frustrated, guilt ridden, and sick at times of himself. Family becomes a burden, confinement, or unnecessary responsibility. Domestic discipline is too harsh for his sensitive ego. Strong frustrations with at least one parent definitely seen here. Dealing with older relatives and inability to create his own domestic discipline causes internal inferiorities. Problems with land, property, real estate can be seen. Career appears insecure but domestic sacrifice uncertain for him. Roots of life harden upon him, enslaving him of the surrounding circumstances. Even though he tries hard not to leave behind the wide family base, he gets caught in the same family tradition. Thus, learning and relearning experiences from family impedence seen in his life. In his previous life, he probably ran away from simple responsibility. Thus, in this life, he has to face it all. To top it all, he has to stick around with long life and depart this world slowly from his own bed.

Life can be secure with only limited outward exposure of achievements. The goal and efforts are needed to evolve out of this with strong ambition, daring and willpower. He has to nurture faith in himself before he can achieve that goal.

Retrograde Saturn Ruling the Fifth House. Challenges in love/romance areas are noticed. Inwardly, there might be a feeling of insecurity but outwardly native appears very bold and action oriented. Dealing with people with age difference can be very significant. Thus, when young, he goes after older person in the relationship and when older, his fascination towards a younger person is seen. Learning and experiencing through relationships can be very important to him in good and bad situations. Sudden emotional freeze, romantic inhibitions, disruptive forceful encounters and repulsive compulsions may be seen in it. A touch of emotional frigidity to total resentment can be present here, but the native outwardly appears much different from reality. Practical sensuality, slow turn-on but intense needs are significant. In a way the native is looking for parental replacement in the situation or trying to be a parent to the other person. Problems, difficulties, sorrows, or confining pressure from children noticed. There is a chance the native may not have children of his own and that in itself can be a serious issue for him. Practical arts, creative but materially oriented hobbies, speculative reversals in gains and an unusual sense of humor seen here. Somehow, the native does not receive sufficient love and affection from father due to various circumstances.

Retrograde Saturn Ruling the Sixth House. Changes in work and services often occur without the native's choice. Clash with superiors seen here as lack of confidence in each other overtakes the required discipline. The native often feels he is getting the short end of the stick as far as work responsibility and compensation are concerned. Hard work efforts need to be put in to achieve required financial returns. Excellent stamina, persistent attitudes and patience shown by him in his work. Often working for a supervisor with key age difference or maturity imbalance seen in this case. Work becomes isolative, monotonous, production oriented and confining. Health may be weaker with problems regarding bones, teeth, joints, skin, hair, knees, etc. Some physical deformation or distortion on the lower right side of the body is significant. Liability, pressure, and responsibility from the mother's side of the family quite potential here. Diet needs proper care and modification. Work discipline backfires upon the native and his responsibilities shift to some other person without his consent. This makes the native frustrative and insecure forcing him to conquer higher success. Work bureaucracies are fluctuating and he has to untangle work politics before he achieves any recognition and success. Learning lessons through own sickness, limitations, and restrictions are seen from somebody around him with the same.

Retrograde Saturn Ruling the Seventh House. Considerable learning experiences from or regarding marriage and partnership noticed here. Spouse might be very insecure, uncertain, and dogmatic about the relationship or the native is very pessimistic and gloomy about it. Cold interactions, frozen emotional exchange, and a sense of duty over rides it all in this case. Marriage is often based upon trust, responsibility, and respect but through indirect way. Here the commitments are not explicit, making the native uncertain about the relationship. Dealing with age and maturity level difference can be very important in it. A lot of drag noticed in the situation, but they survive together inspite of substantial internal friction. Marriage becomes a liability or the spouse could be the hindrance. Delays in marriage or remarriages in older age noticed. The native is very cold and cruel in his objectivity. Sudden fears of depression, isolation, and melancholy attitudes seen here. Grand parental contacts are significant and at times liability or responsibility through them seen. Due to sensitive and touchy nature, the native feels the insensitivity from spouse. In public and social activities, he may enjoy individual freedom. Substantial difference of beliefs, traditions, backgrounds, and cultural interaction seen it. Parental replacement often seen in this marriage or parental influence is very strong in it.

Retrograde Saturn Ruling the Eighth House. Long life or slow departure from life seen here. Sexual inhibitions insecurities, or phobias can be very significant. Individual needs may be suppressed and the partnership is fulfilled on and imaginative fantasizing level. In early life, possible sexual harrasement or deep sexual fears caused by tradition seen here which stay with the native for a long time. Combined resources often create stressful situations or the spouse does not contribute to it as expected. The native can be financially very conservative as to the combined values, even though his perosnal values may be used lavishly. Learning from others' departure, separation or death becomes very important to him with or without choice. Taxes, insurances, credit matters, inheritances could be delayed causing special situations in life. Any expected or anticipated inheritance from the family does not follow the schedule and at times the native may not even get what he deserves. Sexual inhibitions may be caused by one's own inferiorities or lack of self respect in order to fulfill the relationship. A sense of trust, respect, and maturity controls the physical release in this case. fears of confinement or phobias of the unknown are significant that the native has to over come in life. Great patience and persistance exhibited in the growth of common values or combined worth. Home or domestic security is prime objective inspite of other priorities in life.The native enjoys selective environment around him or he is forced to accept that in many cases.

Retrograde Saturn Ruling the Ninth House. Family traditions often represent hindrance to this native. As much as his philosophies and standards are rigid and old fashioned, he finds it necessary to run away from it. Thus, dealing with people of different beliefs, culture, attitudes, or nationality can be important in his life. At the least he will try very hard to isolate himself from his up bringing. Hindrance in higher education or blockages in applying his knowledge for practical use seen.

Seldom he is confident of his convictions, making him introvert, aloof, and self conscious. Problems with legalities, litigations, lack of publicity and recognition seen here. He can be anti-institutional as he fears being lost in the crowd. Stage fright attitude is very likely in this case. Strong fluctuations or departure from standard religion noticed. Needs to travel may be only internal, but actual travel substantially limited. If he gets a chance to travel, long trips do not always bring pleasure to him. Weak father image perceived by him or hidden resentments towards him due to unusual circumstances. When applicable, second marriage can be a complicated issue. Although full of challenges, it can be hard to get away from to be free again.

Retrograde Saturn Ruling the Tenth House. Struggle, hard work and patience seen in his career. He cannot stand his profession, but at the same time he cannot detach from it. This circumstantial bind associated with his career lasts for a while, and then new opportunity emerges. Changes in what he wants to do are noticed careerwise, but eventually, he comes to similar brick wall of dissatisfaction. This lack of satisfaction, provides him with superb ambition and persistance. Difficulties with father or mutual resentments created in the interaction. He has great respect towards father and at the same time father expects a lot out of this native. Competing with father or doing something totally opposite than what he does is seen here. A sense of responsibility and circumstantial pressure are thrust upon the native without asking for it. Family discipline, needs and expectations drive the person for outside achievements. Inferiorities often created in him due to the way elders treat him. Their intentions are good at times to purify and weather him, but the means appear cruel and insensitive to the native. Difficulties, dilemmas and unavoidable challenges from the superiors on the job or just professional bureaucracy seen in here. He is never best suited to be number one in anything. The quest for being at the top of hill may not be fulfilled and finally he accepts that compromise in life. Home-career imbalance is often seen in his life and his ego is maintained flexible by circumstantial force most of the time.

Retrograde Saturn Ruling the Eleventh House Friendships are considered great responsibility here, but often they turn out excessive liability to the native. Frustrations may occur all of a sudden through friends and group associations in his life. As a result, the native tries to be very selective, detached, and picky about them. With all the care, he still ends up with similar output and interactions as the past history. Age difference or muturity level difference needed in this case for better results. Thus, his fascination for the generation just above or below him can be significant as far as social, friendly interactions are concerned. His hopes and goals may be old fashioned and conservative. He is not adventurous most of the time and may not even take significant risks in life. A feeling of unlovedness or neglect from others to him is seen. Thus, he spends time creating his own enjoyment. Resources made through career and profession are very significant as they represent most of his life holdings. He may not discuss his dreams and goals with others due to his inner insecurities and lack of faith within himself.

Retrograde Saturn Ruling the Twelfth House. Fear of the unknown, insecurities from the past and lack of faith within himself are noticed here. Past mistakes often catch up with him which force him to run fast in life. Quite difficult past incarnation noticed for him where he had to suffer for his consequences. Somehow, his punishment was not enough then, and he has to fulfill his Karmic debt in this life time. To compensate for this, he may pretend to be a disbeliever of the law of Karma. Sometimes, his upbringing and early life philosophies forbid him to have such universal faith or esoteric beliefs. However, as time goes on he can be well sold on the universal machine and his role in the cosmos. Hidden fears, internal suffering, or learning from sickness can be important directly or indirectly in his life. Thus, sometimes some one around him undergoes stress, suffering, and problems which affect this native very well. Dealing with older people/relatives, confining situations, institutions, etc. can be important. Superstitious nature inside but adventurous and unique personality outwardly seen. Outward unconventionalities fight strongly with inner conventional nature. His roots of life are shaken up periodically and his subconscious reprogrammed. Learning to establish a balance between security/stability and confinement of life is very crucial here. Forced isolation or independence thrust upon him when he may not want it.

RETROGRADE SATURN OPPOSITE MOON

Emotionally, very sensitive but self-depressive tendencies noticed in this person. Emotions and feelings remain the key areas around which the native has to build his standards and discipline. Thus, any discipline that compromises his emotional stability is rejected. In doing so, the person chooses other means to achieve the same outcome by sacrificing other areas of life. Mothering or nurturing is very important to and from this individual. This emotional pampering is expected or given to others indirectly. Career is often sacrificed for the sake of better home and domestic situations. Thus, the native may not be highly compelled to go out and prove himself at the expense of a shaky home. Insecurities are noticed here but the native may not be aware of them as a problem. Difficulties with mother through early childhood seen. Here mother is highly needed but cannot stand her type of attitude noticed in the interaction. Mother's influence is definitely responsible for the growth of this individual. Other components of the family are not at all significant contributors to him. Family tradition, heritage, and general responsibilities are all kept flexible and at times resented if they get in the way of his own emotional fulfillments. As an outcome the native appears withdrawn, lonely, melancholy, and introverted. Self-evaluation, introspections, and being his own emotional parasite can be noticed here. Many of these inward energies converge to a very productive and useful purpose. Internal purification helps the native substantially in this life time in his own Karmic growth. In a way, this is a very subjective life and he may not outwardly share his life findings with others. Partnerships cause liabilities, difficulties, and strong responsibilities forcing him to run away from it all. He may or may not be successful at that, so he has to stay there and cope with the circumstances. Family responsibility, frustrations through elders and sudden burdens on life occur here that the native has to be prepared for in life. Weaker health, emotional breakdown, improper nourishment potential are likely here.

RETROGRADE SATURN OPPOSITE SUN

Tradition, conservative attitudes and substantial impedence hold the native from achieving a lot of success in the outside world. However, slowly he begins to convert those liabilities into productive assets as the time goes on. Thus, in later years good crystallizing influence is nicely seen in the life of this individual. Sticking to what he believes is right helps him in the long run. Respect for tradition is deeply seen and he is willing to move mountains once he establishes a trust and faith in something. His success is guaranteed as long as he goes by the book and the past established procedure. Conservative support can be behind him once he is ready to do something for the society. Children are very important and the upbringing he provides is excellent. Somehow, in his childhood, he did not get everything he wanted. As a result, he will try to be an ideal parent to his offsprings. Family ties and greater involvements with relatives are seen in his life. However, he really wants to get away from it all. Individual success is important to him, even though family support is unavoidably there. Many changes or sacrifices in his career areas are seen as the native does not find his itch until later in life. He may have to abide by the rules under the superiors until he finds his way out of the situation. In a woman's chart, difficulties with father, men, and masculinity are noticed. Somehow her inhibitions dominate her personality substantially to demand what she wants out of the relationship. Then she just accepts it as a discipline or duty. Resentments gather within and eventually she just does not want any men in her life at all. This, of course, lasts for a short while. Thus, more than one marriage or just the change in confinement noticed here. She is often likely to find a replacement father figure in her husband. Her career or professionalism is important but secondary compared to her spouse. Physiologically, weaker bone structure or boney profile, unusual teeth, skin or hair likely. Long life or slow departure from life noticed here. Persistence, stamina and ability to "hang in there" with patience are definitely seen as far as the end result is to his own advantage. However he may not do that for somebody else.

RETROGRADE SATURN OPPOSITE MERCURY

A strong touch of seriousness associated with the logic and thinking noticed here. As a result, his plans and strategies can be very elaborate, old fashioned, and rigid. Self-repressive tendencies are possible as the native can be pessimistic in spite of his thorough thinking. Lot of efforts and discipline goes in the making of decisions. Here the person reiterates whatever he is going to externalize all within just to be cautious. Rigidity, conservativeness and a sense of antiquity are seen in his mental process. Brother/sister relationships are given much more priority and attention compared to other family relatives. Work is more significant than just the professional goals. As a result, the type of actual service will decide whether he would continue in that type of profession or not. Good concentration ability is seen and the native is apt to go after mental performance rather than pure experiences. He is likely to make the same mistakes again, but he seldom will have to learn and understand the same thing on the mental level. Thus, here the mistakes are just circumstances, wrong guesses or his pure Karma. Family pressure can be strongly an inhibition in his learning. Thus, there might be some discouragements in his learning capability. This could be done as an unfair comparison with his ancestors or others around him, making him feel inadequate of his mental status. Slow but steady progress definitely seen on the job. He is excellent in terms of counselling and providing good advice to others. Delays in travel can be seen but those are not his faults. As a result, the native lacks interest in travel or just moving around. His mannerism is quite unique, unusual, and quiet. He is not likely to display his ambition very well, but he puts his efforts and hopes for the best. Lot of similarities noticed in this individual and the grandparents. Thus, a generational jump in the characters is very unique and significant. Interest in the opposite sex is minimal and a lot of self-love, introversion, and low profile is maintained by the native. It is highly possible that the person may not want a larger family of his own and at times may not have any.

RETROGRADE SATURN OPPOSITE VENUS

Romanticism, personal relationship, and ideology are so strong that nothing gets in his way. As a result, once he decides what he wants in personal situations, you cannot reason with him or give him any practical resistance. The native is willing to compromise and sacrifice his standards, ethics, and sense of basic judgement for the sake of his romantic pursuits. Here money and marriage/partnership issues are so much important compared to his career, profession or life goals. He often goes against the family expectations regarding his choice of mate. In doing so, a lot of family static and hindrance has to be overcome and he has that stamina. Once he gets what he wants, he may not be so pleased with it. Often the spouse differs much in age, maturity, and culture from him and that plays mixed role in keeping them together but with cold wars. Creative, artistic, and talented side is willing to find success in life at the cost of most practical sacrifices. Dealing with older folks, relatives, or just antiquity of family structure is something he resents, but cannot really detach away from. Power of discipline and methodology appears uncertain to him in making the relationship an easy success. As a result, he applies discipline and methodology only to regret and get stuck in his own rules. The constant battle within, as to should he keep the family happy or go after his own happiness. As a result, war erupts between the family and generations. In business partnership, he values the partnership more than the actual business. As a result, his partner may not continue too long in that arrangement, unless the business just gets lucky. People and general public is given more value than the government and the authority figures who control them. Thus, this native can have good success with people but not necessarily in an administrative bureaucracy. Fluctuating learning lessons and complexes with father seen here. Objectivity is more important than self-ego boost. Under pressure he vacillates and has to get help from others. Personal relationships have durability but a lot of sacrificial expectations to keep it going.

RETROGRADE SATURN OPPOSITE MARS

Strong self-confidence noticed without any serious regards for inhibitions. Standards are compromised to get where he wants to be in life. A touch of ruthlessness, stepping on others and adaptability of surrounding structure make this native successful at some point in life. This success may not be durable, but he has the capabilities to maintain his status, if he so chooses. Hard driving character is displayed here and he is willing to take risks at every step of the game. Family, legalities, conservative attitudes and sense of respect do not stand a chance against him as he can be much too determined and self-willed to be stopped by them. He is a leader but he does not like others to follow him. As a result, he can be alone and lonely at many curves of time frames. Authority is significant to him than responsibility. Purpose appears glamorous than goals. 'Energies are to be used rather than disciplined' can be his motto. Going against the family tradition or just not even thinking about where he came from, is noticed here. Impulsiveness can be his worst enemy and no thorough planning is taken into account to do most projects. Cruelistic, sadistic or masochistic tendencies are seen, as he pleasurizes pain and its exchange. He can be a cause of pain and suffering to others but in return he often gets it all back from them. Disruptions, calamities, and abrupt events occur in his early childhood. Feeling of humility can be noticed here that provides him the ambition to prove himself later in life. Accident prone tendencies, sexual distortions can be likely. In a female chart, unusual male identity is seen in the close personal relationship. Love/hate combinations or mutually punishing attitudes are displayed. They love each other but certainly they have unusual ways to show their affection. Complexities in the relationship with brother/sister can be seen here. Some unusuality regarding brother-in-law or sister-in-law can be very likely. Self-depression to make himself happy is noticed here as an unusual human character. Some social and cultural problems are created by him or the native becomes the victim of such situations.

RETROGRADE SATURN OPPOSITE JUPITER

Strong struggle regarding the social values, individual orientation, and practicality of philosophies is notice in this native. Somehow beliefs, ideology, and philosophies survive, giving practicality and materialism a day off. This tension between material and the non-material is very common to this person; and as the times goes on, he simply philosophizes the entire life. He has to deal with mundane practicality and build a strong resistance to them in order to grow on the esoteric path. Theory is much more important than the actual practicality or statistic in this case. People and relatives away from home can be significant in his life, than just the close family living with him. Discipline is often compromised here to achieve something supernatural by virtue of strong faith. Education signifies worth in this case rather than simple practical experience. Through early childhood, he had to consolidate his elder's commands and wishes into something of a philosophical ideology. He is much better to serve a goal rather than an order. Due to fluctuating or inconsistent discipline in the family, he seldom makes a good parent. However, his children can look up to him for his optimism, futurism, and success in life. It is likely that he may not have a large family of his own as through early childhood he learns what a child has to go through to grow up to be an adult. Education, philosophies, and institutional attraction is strong making this native sacrifice some of his professional goals. Thus, the profession has to lead him to a better human philosophy, or it should have a large organizational structure. Thus, self-employment or very rare professions are seldom chosen by this individual. He can be morbid at times, but he has a good reason to be so under certain circumstances. He resents poverty, suffering, and loss of individual freedom, as he may be there at times within his life. However, his lucky stars will pull him out of those slumps eventually. For good moral standards and what he believes in, he can sacrifice social justice and even go against social norms.

RETROGRADE SATURN OPPOSITE URANUS

A strong conflict of conventionality and unconventionality is noticed in this native. However, the outcome is very unique and unconventional. Due to circumstances, he is often stripped off from his standards, attitudes and rigid behavior. It is like shaking him away from the mold he was cast into this life time. He has great attraction, admiration, and respect for his family tradition. However, due to events in his life, he is forced to drift away from that all. Family sacrifice is done here in order to prove himself unique and unusual in life. Breaking away from the norm becomes his goal no matter where it leads him in life. Innovation, inventiveness and ability to take chances are quite strong in his life as the time goes on. In life, he often reforms himself to something that attracts him. Although he has strong built-in discipline within himself, he takes pride in achieving things without indulging in any format, structure, or methodology. Irregularly regular character seen here. Rebelliousness by virtue of past confinements or just the idea of its reality noticed in this combination. Friendships are preserved and valued on the job. Career or profession can be sacrificed or compromised for the sake of maintaining the friendships and group associations. Clash with father is noticed as their goals certainly differ in the light of generational difference. Pursuit of achieving something new, different, or unique is so important that he may give up his practical, conventional, and secure life style. Sensation overrides security in this case. The native may go through some social problems, sudden confinements or obstruction of justice during his life. He does so to prove himself unique, different or just for his new philosophy. Esoteric interests, metaphysical attractions, and new social values are very important and significant to him. For that reason, he utilizes his efforts, stamina, discipline, and resources. For the sake of new dawn, he is willing to give up his comfortable water bed and wait out in the rainly environment. Here pleasure of that new arrival outweighs any compromises he may do.

RETROGRADE SATURN OPPOSITE NEPTUNE

The search for practical dreams is underway in this case. The person wants to forget, wipe out, or neglect any serious practicality getting in his way of achieving his things. This sacrifice of materialism for the sake of idealism seen here. However, once they catch up with their rainbow, they realize that the colors have been distorted. New search begins and new compromises undertaken. As a result, it is hard for this native to be financially and materially successful over a long period. A willingness to give up security and good experiences in the hope of greener grass ahead in the future is seen here. Family traditions are strong but lessons have to be learned to put them in different perspective of the esoteric life. Creativity or imagination is excellent along with appropriate instincts and gut feelings. Ideology is quite strong that forgets the practical reality of any existing situations. A secret or hidden respect towards father or any authority shown, but the native indulges in abiding by the supreme nature, and naturalism. Standards are meant to be flexible and here the person enjoys breaking his own rules. There may not be any serious immorality in his doing so, but the happiness derived through that escapement is plentiful. Any restrictions, confinements or pressured areas are rebelled away, utilizing the powers of imagination, fantasies, and make-believe situations. At times this escapism could be from his own phobias, inhibitions, and inner insecurities. Strong belief in Karma, life after death, reincarnation is possible here as means to explain certain experiences. Future can be very important to this native and he is willing to forget the past easily. Past often becomes a liability to him as the temptations created by the tradition are hard to resist to achieve the glamorous future. Hidden activities, complex dealings with government, institutions, or bureaucracy likely in this case. On a physical level, some malfunctions in bones, teeth, hair, or general health areas noticed. Family is very important to the native in early life, but then he suddenly detaches from it to resolve his life goals.

RETROGRADE SATURN OPPOSITE PLUTO

Rebellious and antiestablishment attitude seen that has serious, practical, and rigid bases. The native wants to go against the social norms just to get attention and individual kicks. Tradition is often sacrificed or at times ruthlessly rejected in the hope of better reform for life. Masses and the society become more important than simple family and nearby surroundings. Going against the father, authority, or any discipline noticed. The native resent any pressure from the nearby close environment for the ideological growth in the social movement. Restructure in basic beliefs, standards, and life concepts definitely seen. There are some under-currents relating to career-profession areas. At times, the native may even give-up normal practical work to go into the underground economy. Metaphysical, psychological, or mystical interests compel him to give up his life skepticism and be more aware of the universal sensitivity. A lot of power-play strategy noticed in the family interactions; and he can be the black sheep of the family. He respects others or authority but not through the average means. This respect is towards the underdog appeal or towards something that can promise social, economical and institutional restructure. He loves to lobby against the tradition and social conservativeness. Individuality is not important as long as enough others share his unusual dream to achieve the desired goals. Dealing with hidden resources, credit matters, taxes, and socio-legal reforms can be significant here. Work involving with institutions, research, and investigation can be important. Disintegration for the sake of consolidation seen. Foundations are weakened in order to know more under the surface. Thus, motivations are much more significant than simple law and order. Here the law is broken in order to bring better justice and order in life.

RETROGRADE URANUS

The retrograde uranus brings out the uranian qualities more significantly. Thus, unusual uniqueness, freedom of independence and inventive brilliance can be portrayed here. Attention seeking mechanism works in this case by reverse process. The native may not seek publicity or any attention consciously. However, due to his actions, attitudes and what he does not do, bring a focus upon him. His eccentricity might be taken as new approach or fashion of the time. Isolation, seclusion, independence and loneliness are all seen here with or without his choice. Social attitudes are much different from others but he definitely needs socializing with unique class of people. Sometimes, it occurs so unexpectedly, he hardly has a choice to select his association. He is often catagorized in a special classification by virtue of his behavior, attitude and personality. He will put up a fight for freedom and independence. However after getting what he wants, he becomes restless because others diffuse away from him. Thus, independence is needed without isolation by his unique thinking. Innovative and inventive sides of his personality isolate him from a commoner. This creates a perfectionistic inventor. This challenge to his own creation produces good results in the long run. General rebellious attitude, resentment towards conventionality and a sense of self propelled destiny seen here. There are times he does not want to be unique, different and unusual. However, others place him in that classification. He cannot fight the social views or attitudes, eventually becoming what others thought he was. Many changes in friendships are seen in this case. Need to experiment, involve and evolve, gather universal understanding, etc., are quite significant for this native. A search for goal is always on without really knowing the goal. "I will know when I find it" attitude seen regarding the classical rainbow of hopes in this case. He can be sympathetic but may not be sensitive. Regularity and punctuality occur with irregularity giving others different opinions about himself. Humanitarian sense is within him, but it cannot be relied upon at all the times. Moodiness overtakes him instantly, making him a much different personality all of a sudden. Keeping an eye on future gives him confidence to go after things However, he often neglects the present, which eventually changes his projected future.
As a result, his hopes, goals and wishes undergo modifications and even total reversals at times in the long run. Fluctuating mannerism, unpredictable and inconsistent responses but generally exciting personality seen here. One shot deals are important, as the native does not care for repetition and monotomy. General carefree attitude but a strong inner sense of goals are seen here.

RETROGRADE URANUS THROUGH THE HOUSES

Retrograde Uranus in the First House — Innovative, unusual, temperamental and self destructive, wild beginnings and abrupt endings, escapist, independence seeking, free-floating and carefree, changeable moods and unique reactions, identifies well in the crowd, unpredictably predictable, expects and demands special treatment from others, detached and dissociative, fond of travel, variety of friends and special interest groups, self recognition inherited rather than acquired, diffused exits, anti-monotonous, non traditional.

Retrograde Uranus in the Second House — Unique money making ideas, romantic worth much different than others, material innovations, valuable inventions, unique approaches, personality changes in mid-third part of life, fluctuating finances, attitudes vary a lot regarding personal worth, demands financial independence, values freedom, worthy of carefree character, unique eye sight or eye movement, mother's involvement in unusual group associations, financial difference with spouse, uncommonly practical.

Retrograde Uranus in the Third House — Mental kinks, ability for independent thinking, antisocial or does not agree with the nearby society, wants to be totally different from brothers and sisters, black sheep of the family at all costs, takes complex way out, mental brightness, innovation of ideas, nervous, hyper and abruptly expressive, learns through intuition, mental experimentations, likes to travel to new places, unconventional mannerism, hysteria inherited from mother's side, anti-regulations, much different in intelligence from his class of students, opinionated.

Retrograde Uranus in the Fourth House — unusual early life, rebellious at home, anti-security conscious, unique relationship with mother due to circumstances or by her attitudes, likes to leave home early in life, domestic discipline does not agree with him, goes against the family tradition, needs sensationalism at home, pleasurises in unique surroundings, unexpected benefits or loss through home, lands, property, etc. Inventive at home but disruptive hysteria shown, abnormal habits and different lifestyle seen. Roomy home, unusual family spirits scatter at home, talks to himself at home.

Retrograde Uranus in the Fifth House — Unconventional, exceptional and unusual in love/romance, needs freedom and individuality in the relationship, willingness to experiment with nontraditional things, holds no bars, carefree pursuits and noncommital attitudes in romance. Fluctuating interests in children, basic needs are much different than others. Special talents, creativity and chances taken in life. Risks things without consequences, unusual and bizzare attracts him the most and fast, unconventional life sought after, detached feelings. Eccentricity is an asset or others like that quality in him.

Retrograde Uranus in the Sixth House — Many changes in jobs, hates monotony, creative and productive towards custom items, disagrees with coworkers, nerve gathering, unusual and different work habits or schedules, does not like set patterns, refuses to be classified on the job, very uncommon relatives on the mother's side of the family, rebelliousness at work and nervous tantrums displayed, carefree towards life security, intellectual but kinky ideas executed, unusual health and diet, nervous disorders, improper reflexes & circulatory imbalances, likes innovation but dislikes maintenance and responsibility, less than perfection shown.

Retrograde Uranus in the Seventh House — Unusual attractions and always in search of unique partnerships, more than one marriage, fluctuating objectivity, spouse becomes unreliable and at times untrustworthy, special socializing needed to please the native, enjoys politics but may not participate in it, social image can be unpredictable, unique standards of life, sensation seeking, exciting casual relationships work the best, carefree and independence seeking attitude displayed by the partner, unexpected anti-social behavior.

Retrograde Uranus in the Eighth House — Uncommon sensational needs, diffused sexuality, physical drive transformed into something different, occult interests, metaphysical attractions, unusual sexual behavior and needs, enjoys special relationship with free interchange, eccentricity as an asset socially, different than others, unexpected gains from combined values or through other's resources, idealism towards marriage creates far and few opportunities in between. Unique turn ons and bizzare personal life experiences, mystical attractions.

Retrograde Uranus in the Ninth House — Rebellious philosphies, success away from birth place, long trips and travel seen, enjoys mystical-occult beliefs, delays or unexpected blocks in higher education, unconventional second marriage, freedom of personalities binds the actual relationship, relatives away from home base cause concern, legal battles or ligitations likely, problems with offsprings or dealing with other's children. Unusual health history to mother, unexpected turning points in one's life beliefs and standards.

Retrograde Uranus in the Tenth House — Career fluctuations and sudden departures noticed. Difficulty getting along with superiors, independence and self employment are possible, uncommon father or father image much different than expected. Reactions unpredictable under pressure. Image in the society is very unique and uncommon, drives for power using unconventional means, non traditional practicality, ego shown through uniqueness of individuality, exceptional faith in himself.

Retrograde Uranus in the Eleventh House — Changeable friendships, drifts in and out of group associations, wants to be uniquely identified by friends, strives for self image that is universially different. Unique situations turn him on, love received has to be in unconventional format. Problems with offspring or other's children. Financial ideas clash with father or superiors, innovative goals more important than common means, idealism, independence and carefree soul gain prominance in life achievements. Take it or leave it attitude with friends. Unexpected career changes in mid-third part of life.

Retrograde Uranus in the Twelfth House. Resists isolation and confinement with rebellion, underdog appeal, works behind-the-scene to prepare his uniqueness. Humanitarian, fantasizes and visualizes his special creation, gets high on himself, circumstantial confinements force him to be a loner, inventive perceptions, talented arts & creative ideals, complex subconscious, weird dreams, bizzare fantasies actually mentally constructed in conscious mind. Quite unique past life and dealings with misused occult and mysticism.

RETROGRADE URANUS RULING THE HOUSES

Retrograde Uranus Ruling the First House. The native has a lot to learn about his own personality. Sometimes he wonders why he does things the way they come out. Reactions, reflexes and initiatives are very unpredictable. Self efficiency is often demanded by the native, but others see that as eccentricity by convenience. Getting attention for things he did not do or did not intend to do is seen here. He does not show a sense of responsibility but deep within him, he knows his destiny. If that responsibility and his hidden destiny coincide, he will gladly take that pressure upon his shoulders. Individual freedom is needed but he gets that by unusual means. Moody, fluctuating and unreliable tendencies are possible here, but the native becomes a sensational spark to others. Providing innovative inspiration to others can be his direct goal. Traditional, conventionality and rigid practicality can be the areas he runs from. He has to decide who his friends can be rather than others choosing him for their friend. He enjoys characterization, individuality recognition and personal uniqueness in his interactions. Sudden beginnings but abrupt endings seen in his life.

Retrograde Uranus Ruling the Second House. Financial fluctuations and periodic uncertainities highly seen here. The native changes his material and non-material attitudes quite frequently. It may be his choice or circumstantial pressure forces him to do so. Values and resources show him the widest spectrum of pain to pleasure. The native will acquire resources ultilizing innovative, unusual and unique means. However, his ideas backfire upon him. If not careful, his inventions or ideas bring him stormy situations financially. His attitudes towards values and possessions are quite humanitarian and universally connected. Thus, something within him guides him rather than pure logic, towards the material decision making. Resources and material things do not always equate security for him. Thus his ideas for money and values differ substantially from what his security needs can be. Basically, he can be practical, cautious, conservative, and tradition seeking individual. However, family expectations and his goals may not agree. At times, he shows irresponsible behavior just to display his disagreement and rebelliousness towards the family tradition. His ideas, inventions, mental brilliance and special telepathic communicative thinking help him acquire values and worth in this life time.

Retrograde Uranus Ruling the Third House. Due to unusual mentality, the native has uncommon interactions with the surrounding people. The relationship with brother-sister can be affected in this situation or its total void in his life. Mind works on a different level in this case with extremes of intelligences. Peculiar communication, expression and learning habits are noticed here which are very natural for this native and not necessarily attention seeking from others. Surrounding environment often reacts abnormally to this native forcing him to reciprocate in the same fashion to others. Unexpected travel, exciting journeys, but unpredictable end results seen in his life. A unique angle of attack or thinking seen in him as to achieve the objective. Here the logic works in most illogical way or others have hard time comprehending his logical perspectives. Some uniqueness or abnormality regarding using his hands and hearing capabilities seen. Innovation, inventiveness, and intuitive capabilities can be significant. Some problems, difficulties, or misunderstandings in early school age learning are likely. If not, his performance is often underrated.

Retrograde Uranus Ruling the Fourth House. Some domestic peculiarities or feeling of being in the wrong family seen here. There is nothing wrong with either of them, just a mismatched attitude on the native's side. The family provides everything in their capacity to the native, but he is tuned to something different in life, not realizing their contributions for his growth. Unusual relationship with mother, with a high intuitive communicative link seen here. He wants to break away from the family tradition just to be different. However, he does not remain so unique after he changes his life style. After all, he is still the same individual he was. Transfer of life roots does not change his personality, rather his interactions and reciprocity with the surrounding environment. A sense of security fluctuates, making it hard for him to settle down. Once he settles down, he wants something different for his life goals. It is hard for this individual, consciuosly or unconsciously, to see himself in a long family tree emerging from him. He may be romantic, idealistic, and possessive in a close relationship; but often a very small family structure is seen for him. Benefits through property, real estate or family inheritance are quite unpredictable and at times, he gets the short end of the bargain in them. Unusual domestic discipline, living standards and family interactions are noticed in this case.

Retrograde Uranus Ruling the Fifth House Exciting, unusual, but sensational attitudes towards love/romance seen. The native is fascinated by the unique, uncommon and unusual challenge for his personal interaction. Thus, he may go after things which standout or "turn him on" on a different wave length. A need to experiment, experience or derive sensation can be very strong. Introductory offers fascinate the native, but he cannot take long term advantage of any situation. He needs freedom, independence, and individuality in his interactions. No strings, attached or no serious emotional manipulation noticed here. A sense of responsibility is minimal. As a result, he may not want larger family and especially children. Unique but inventive creativity seen here. The native can actually put his soul into the creative expressions, making them very appealing and interesting. A tendency towards distorted relationships, degenerative interactions, or even bizzare stimulations possible. Monotony gets to him in life and for that reason, his search towards perpetual stimuli continues. Unusual luck in speculation seen here, but that is something the native cannuot count upon all the time. Creative energies, when used properply in this case, can make the native popular, famous and recognized.

Retrograde Uranus Ruling the Sixth House. Fluctuating work attitudes seen here. The native needs a lot of freedom, independence and isolation on the job. As a result he is best suited for self-employment or work that provides him his own boss. It is hard for the native to get along with coworkers as his philosphies, expectations and mannerisms to achieve the objectives are much different from them. Unusual work schedules, timetable and work surroundings seen here. The native needs to be uniquely defined in his profession. For that reason, he will change, quit, modify or even create new jobs and careers. He wants recognition without the responsibility on the job. Often his work and professional objectives differ. Thus at one point he works hard to make money in order to sustain himself while invests towards his profession. Unusual diet or eating habits are noticed. Minor circulatory problems or imbalanced circulation seen in this case. Quite unusual mother's side of the family noticed here or interactions with them are very uncommon. A hidden sensation in marriage often expected or the native feels uneasy about the hidden phobias in marriage. Unique talent or thinking on a job has to be used in this case.

Retrograde Uranus Ruling the Seventh House Fluctuating and flexible objectivity seen here. What native wants from others and what he gets can be considerably different. His opinions regarding others change as he gets to know them deeper. Fascination for the people of opposite personality is seen here. As a result, his spouse will be much different than him regarding age, physical appearance, maturity, and social status, etc. In many instances, spouses will be much out of his balance, but the relationship can be very strong for a while. More than one marriage or total change in mutual attitudes often seen here. It occurs due to both parties getting bored with the same thing over a period of time. They often out grow each other looking for new exchange of interaction and sensation. Often it is the spouse who causes this initiation rather than the native. In-laws are often responsible for widening the gap in this union. His social life can reach either extremes. Thus, he can be super extroverted and socially oriented or just isolative type. Problems with marital freedom, mutual possessiveness and an undefined sense of responsibility are seen. Strange offsprings or sudden responsibility of nephews and nieces can be likely in this case. Attention seeking but touchy personality noticed.

Retrograde Ruling the Eighth House Strong interest in the occult, metaphysics or just the unknown noticed here. Very curious attitude and need to know about others give him excellent sense of perceptions and intuitiveness. Very unique and unusual things turn him on and his true sensations come from the most unusual sources. Quite fluctuating libido or sexual interests vacillate periodically. Combined resources can be uncertain as both parties may not truly contribute towards it consistently. Thus, one works and the other one enjoys the together funds. This creates sudden animosity and combined values get individualized. His attitudes towards death, life after death and reincarnation are very unique and fascinating. Fear of the unknown is stronger to him than the fear of death of the physical body. He is able to control his sexuality for the sake of transcending it to a high form of energy. He may or may not be aware of the process in doing so. Unexpected complications, delays, or crucial learning experiences seen from inheritance and others' resources. He can be very individualistic, sensitive and emotional but his attitudes towards masses and larger groups are very opposite. Potential complex situations with step-brothers/sisters are possible in this case.

Retrograde Uranus Ruling the Nineth House The native experiences wide range of philosphies, cultures and beliefs. Universal awareness touches him contantly making him shape up his life philosphy in proper format. He may have difficulty, delays, or anxiety in distant places. As a result, relocations are not quite smooth and easy for him. Although he can encounter cultural changes and show adaptability, he has difficulty diffusing his identity. Thus, he remains solid and stubborn towards what he is and what he was. When applicable, second marriage causes much more problems than the first one. Here the first partner needed more freedom and independence than him. As a result, he idealizes his second relationship to be much different than the first. However, reality shakes him up with a repeat experience. In legal matters, the outcomes have a tendency to nosedive at the last minute. However, he receives unusual publicity from it as a compensation. Delays or frustrations in higher education are likely or the actual learning experiences become useless for practical applications. Getting involved with different religion, institutions or group activity seen here.

Retrograde Uranus Ruling the Tenth House Unusual career and professional interests noticed here. The native needs free-floating regime in his careers. In demanding so, he often has to sacrifice generous conservative fringe benefits. Sudden and abrupt changes can be expected in the career direction which actually provide periodic sensation to the native. He may not take serious responsibility on the job. However, once he commits himself to a belief, he will be pretty stable and consistent with it. Under pressure, he reacts very unpredictable, rebellious and verbally disruptive. He will argue with most far-fetched logic to get himself out of the jam. The relationship with father or authority is unusual. A deep sense of respect covered with basic disagreements seen here. Somehow the generational gap is too wide to bridge or the conventionalities differ in attitudes in this case. Goals of life are achieved using unconventional, inventive and unique means. The native tumbles periodically in attaining his goals, but he can be persistent with his belief to achieve the objective. His social image may be distorted even though he is sympathetic to his friends. Somehow, he has to compete with his father's image or totally go opposite of his achievements.

Retrograde Uranus Ruling the Eleventh House. Friendships are formed quickly but they diffuse easily. A sense of fascination attracts him towards others, but the glamor or sensation fades away easily. As a result, the residual friendships hinge upon the humanitarian link. At least one of them have to feel sorry, apathy, or sympathy towards the other. Fluctuating hopes and goals of life force the native to drift around maintaining his monotonous career. Often his career is stable, secure but boring, which does not give him a chance to explore other sensations in his mind. The love received from others can be abrupt, unreliable, and fluctuating. Thus, even though he is very giving in live emotions, he does not get proper share back from others. Of course, his expectations are much different from others as far as the anticipation of love received is concerned. Social encounters, unusual group association, music, arts, unconventional gatherings all turn him on. His participation in those things can be great learning sources for him. Experimenting with friends seen here, but things backfire upon him abruptly. Financial support from father can be very uncertain for him.

Retrograde Uranus Ruling the 12th House A sense of spiritual destiny and need to be do something to get ahead of everbody in that game seen here. The native will take chances in his balance of material and non-material achievements in life. Thus, he can justify climbing the material ladder to achieve non-material purity. "Substance" can be used to conquer the spirit and philosophy is used very well be this native. Life fantasies, vivid dreams, amd most unusual events in dreams are seen. Behind-the-scene activities or underdog appeal can produce most devilish thinking. Escapement tendencies or run away attitudes use quite inventive means. High strong and nervous nature under isolative conditions seen. He is not certain about his past life as to whether he directed it properly or not. As a result, he often repeats his life, just in case, he did not complete the mission in the past. He is afraid of hypnosis or anyone probing his subconscious. He shows superstitions, detachments from friends and suppressed temper tantrums. Excellent psychic communication with father likely, but difficulties with his side of family noticed.

RETROGRADE URANUS OPPOSITE MOON

Moody and unpredictable behavior constantly seeks emotional excitement. Emotional nervous energy is substantially wasted or consumed within. If used properly and constructively, this energy can work wonders. Touchy behavior and high strongness are associated with this condition. Problems, difficulties but periodic excitement often seen with women and femininity. Unusual means are used in the interactions with people around. Domestic security is valued considerably more than just large group associations or friends. Emotional inventiveness is seen here that provides various possible means of expressions of feelings. It is hard to get along with mother, but one has difficulty moving away from her. This duality causes stress in the personal life goals later. Hysteria or emotional explosions are used to get the individual attention he needs. Family heritage is very important but the native will seek out various outside means to boost his status in life. Personal goals and hopes are often sacrificed to keep the key woman in life happy and content. Artistic, creative talents are used in connections with mass media. Uniqueness becomes an added asset and depth to his personality. However, overly done eccentricity brings him emotional turmoil. Need for nurturing is in focus and at all possibilities, he would want that. Imagination can be very vivid, but he resents anyone disrupting his such escapment. He has to spend a lot of time and energies to get his inner insecurities to normalization. Emotional phobias or emotional breakdown potential is likely. However, at that time, he has to sacrifice his friendships and group associations. He recovers better on his own with peace and tranquility rather than increased interpersonal exchange.

RETROGRADE URANUS OPPOSITE SUN

Freedom or independence is compromised in order to evaluate one's own standing in the surrounding environment. Self is more important as to what others see in you rather than your own perceptions. Unusual means are utilized to gain self-respect and individual boost. Sense of respect towards an authority is shown but through much uncommon behavior. Imbalance in love exchange is noticed as the native is uncertain to grasp the true love received from others. Friendships and group associations create complex circumstances in the life of this individual. As long as he contains his uniqueness and unusuality to himself, he is fine. However, when that gets projected upon others, his uncommonness becomes a problem issue. He requires and demands enough free space around him, but at the same time he resents void or emptiness surrounding him. Respect for father is shown by him, but through his own way. Quite creative talents are noticed here, which can bring good success in life. Friendships are sacrificed for romance as he can find more friends whenever he chooses to do so. Lack of children is often likely. However, he will put significant efforts in their proper cultivation if he has any offspring. He values his home, stability, and roots of life in a very inner but special way. What others see in him is much different than his own perspectiveness in that case. Unpredictable temperament and sudden attacks of introversion are seen. Early separations, detachments, or unusual events occur in the family. In a woman's chart, this often indicates quite unique and uncommon male figure in life. Her attractions are much more different than what she can be compatible in the actual relationship. Mischievous tendencies are quite likely as the person needs attention at all costs. Publicity, good or bad, is often received in this case.

RETROGRADE URANUS OPPOSITE MERCURY

Innovative, unique, and unusual ideas crowd the mind. Mental focus is constantly applied to everything. Outwardly, it may not seem so as the nervous energies often dominate the good, clean cut ideas. Planning becomes more important in terms of its detailed execution rather than pure inventiveness. Ideas on the lower practical domain are given priorities compared to brilliant but far-fetched ones.

Practicality and down-to-earth applications are quickly favored by this individual. External presentation is significant compared to its inner intricacy. Brother/sister and near environment are much favored compared to friendships. As a result, this individual has more family cohesiveness or together spirit rather than outside friendship interactions. Home surroundings are more influential to him than the worldly neighbor. Slow but steady success in lower education is seen. The value of education depends upon its true work applications. Thus, seldom he would want to be overly educated. Learning and relearning experiences provided from his group associations tend to make him isolated from them as the time goes on. He becomes anti-social not by his choice but due to his reactions to others. Mental alertness is significant and he enjoys keeping up with the inventive state of the art. Short trip or travel nearby is preferred as compared to extensive long journeys. A touch of uniqueness is noticed in his mannerism which helps a great deal in his work, services and communication. Control on nerves is needed and he has to learn to relax to achieve his goals. Rebelliousness is suppressed within but it finds its way through his ideas, communications, and work. Unique sense of services expected by him from others. He is willing to provide and receive good mental exchange all the time. Cultural emphasis is strong compared to just being a black sheep in the family.

RETROGRADE URANUS OPPOSITE VENUS

Unusual experiences surround the person's love life in this situation. Uncommon means, ideas and expectations are noticed to get the desired sensation in personal romances. Unique turn-on's seen here as the native is after something extra ordinary to fulfill his sensational quench. Ultra romantic, innovative approach is quite possible in this case, but he gets turned off easily as well. Money and marriage areas are given considerable priorities once the individual consolidates all his love-received spectrum. Friendship and social interactions are secondary after he achieves his romantic worth. Creative, artistic, and imaginative talents are well cultivated here. The native uses uncommon and unique means to achieve his goals in life as far as acquiring the personal values and pleasures. Women or dealing with them can be highly fluctuating, unpredictable, and at times crazy. Vivid fantasy becomes a periodic substitution for his enjoyments. He demands and expects aloofness from others on the surface, but he can seldom stay away from socializing. His ideas regarding partnerships can be dualistic and even full of double standards. He values and pleasurizes women. As a result, he may not want to be tied down with just one person. In a woman's chart, unusual romances are expected and she is ready for different encounters. Something special is always needed to keep her happy. Here the person vacillates between the spouse and friends. However, at the end the friends are compromised and group associated dissolved. Unique mannerism and approach attracts many people to this individual, but he enjoys the game of tease with them. Idealism is important for him, and he is willing to try a complex path to find an easy way out of life. Fickleness or temporary changeability of moods can be his worst enemies.

RETROGRADE URANUS OPPOSITE MARS

Individuality and self-assertiveness are achieved at whatever the means available to this person. Self gratitude and self significance are quite important. Temper tantrums, high strongness, and attacks of impulsive behavior noticed periodically. Many friendships and group participations are seen with a lot of fluctuations. Goals change constantly or the native reacts abruptly to any circumstantial hindrance in his way to achieve things. Irrationalism needs control but the native indulges in such personality profile. Here today, gone tomorrow attitude seen in this case as to the basic life foundations. Fighting spirits, energies, and stamina are substantial here making the person successful quickly at some point in life. He can use his contacts, friendships, and associations very well to gain superiority in his own life status. Unconventional means, innovative talent, and superior energy quotient are all feasible in here to cultivate grand execution of dreams. Domestic disruptions occur or the native feels itchy at any stable conditions at home. As a result, the person has needs and compulsions to bring excitement through domestic restructure or just changes. Nervous excess needs control as the native is likely to be accident prone and can make abrupt blunders. Sexuality profile requires unusual stimulation and nothing average satisfies him. There is always some force, anger temper, or pressure that excites him the most. Under calm and quiet situations he just does not feel comfortable. In a female chart, multiple marriages or unusual romantic encounters are noticed. Unique sensation requires sudden revival in interests making life quite different from average. Danger from fire, accident, rash, fever, or abrupt explosive situations are possible. Female fertility cycle can be very unpredictable here creating unusual results regarding the offspring situation. Get-even temperament and social injustice are present here making the individual quite uncommon in his search for ideal social environment.

RETROGRADE URANUS OPPOSITE JUPITER

Beliefs, standards, and philosophies remain the key issues around which this person manipulates his variance of ideas. He utilizes his unique talent and applications to find better life standards. He is willing to check and readjust his basic life philosophies in the light of growing internal needs for uniqueness. In most cases, his upbringing dominates the rebellious side, thus leaving inside suppressed hostilities towards the family. He understands the family roots, structure, and so called discipline, but he fails to convince others why he has to remain unchanged. His uniqueness and innovation can be significant helping him be successful in his career, politics, institutional matters, legalities, and even in education. Friends bring him required learning perspectives and he can take good lessons through their interactions. Indecisions and uncertainties as to what route to follow as the road to success is noticed. His stand on religion gets modified by his own ideas. Success and stability in life are important but he finds his stands much different from the spouse. Thus, both have to work towards their goals through different medias. High philosophical ideology and great inspiration for the cosmos are noticed here. However, the individual has to come up with exceptional means and interpretations for his true inner instincts. This interpretive mechanism may appear far-fetched at times to others, but his achievements can be significant in the desired areas. Self-suffering or even sacrificing one's hopes/goals of life is noticed just to get on the band wagon that goes to the heaven. In certain instances, orthodox tendencies, religious rebellion, and even agnostics is noticed here. Complex situations can arise out of legalities and institutional matters. In such cases, the individual takes upon himself heavy burdens with great faith in the universality. Fluctuations in friendships are seen as he has to sacrifice some of the friendships for his personal life stand. However, later on he feels guilty of his past actions and cultivates the same friendships again. In a group oriented activity, he can certainly be much different than others. Distant travel activities or people of different cultural backgrounds are very important in his life focus.

RETROGRADE URANUS OPPOSITE SATURN

Conventionality and unconventionality fight within the indivdual and eventually his conservative side wins. He is often shaken up by unusual circumstances and challenges, but his basic stable structure can take the pressures. Rationalities are more important to him than irrationalities and unconventional situations. He wants to maintain the tradition but at the same time he is willing to look into "Pandora's Box." Career can be an important issue compared to just social recognition without explicit efforts. Friendships come in handy to this individual as they help him achieve success within his professional area. Outwardly, he is calm and collective which indicates considerable internal nervousness. He has an unique way of showing respect to others in the authority. Clashes with father or male dominance is possible, but sooner or later the person understands the other side of the story. Responsibilities are very important and the native is willing to carry them through, no matter what the circumstances which surround them. Family cohesion is a key to his success as he understands their support behind him. Friendships can be sacrificed or altered by this person to get what is desired. Unorthodoxical situations arise in life which he can face very comfortably. Respect for an authority is seen here, hoping he will be in that position someday. Skepticism can be well visible here and the native does not truly believe in any other senses than the usual ones. Short cuts or easy ways have to be proven before he accepts them. Unemotional side of this person helps him in decision making quite nicely. Position with government, authority, or any bureaucratic environment is quite likely here. Precision and practicality become significant compared to artistic or creative, judgement. Harsh and disciplined nature can fight strongly with immorality and social distortions within himself. He may use uncommon means to achieve that, but outwardly he will subscribe to rigid standards. Past activities always catch up to him but often with pleasant outcome. Unusual reflexes, bone, teeth, hair, etc., are quite possible here.

RETROGRADE URANUS OPPOSITE NEPTUNE

Spiritual orientation and esoteric pursuits are clearly noticed in this generation. Understanding the past to help clarify the future is seen in this case. Technological progress is given second priority as compared to the advancement on a worldly level. Instincts and gut feelings are quite superior compared to innovative and genious logic. Mental process works best here on symbology rather than pure deductive reasoning. Unusual, unique, and uncommon fascinate this individual but the trend is to enjoy one's own fantasies without explicit efforts. Make-believe situations, emotional projections, and fabulous acting talents are seen here, even though within himself he is opposed to it all. Hidden activities, past unfinished connections, and a sense of psychological evaluation hound them a lot. Learning and relearning experiences through complex friendships seen here. Misunderstandings, disillusionment and even deceits are quite possible with interactions with others. Many of these personalities undergo considerable changes in their early life. A strong sense of being is established and they almost get possessed by their life dreams. They enjoy secrecy and being a slave of something pleasant in life. Fantasies can be far-fetched as their vivid imagination locks them in a closet. Responsibility and social glamour are not significant and attractive to them. Life is spent in the search of meaning rather than for a purpose. Usually they do not like group associations unless they happen to be involving religion, theatrical experiences, musical, or artistic types. Escapement tendencies are given priorities compared to finding perfect solutions to the situations. They would rather detach and vacate situations instead of implementing new efforts to unlink them. Individual freedom or independence is not truly justified in this generation. Rebelliousness is looked down upon for this individual due to stricter esoteric standards of the mankind. One can only achieve the free-floating states in their own fantasies and make-believe circumstances. Social reforms are seen here only as a mean for individual coexistance for better spirituality. Morality is embedded inside this individual deeply because the social fluctuations seem to take their affects on this generation.

RETROGRADE URANUS OPPOSITE PLUTO

Considerable power play and counter stragies are seen in this generation. Complex pursuits, ideas, and methodology are utilized here to get ahead in life. Challenges and struggles can be a constant dose for them. In spite of this, they hide all their strategies, scars and even outcomes. Outwardly, their life will appear so full of events, but in reality they go through a lot of testing by circumstances. They have very smart minds, innovative thinking, and unique approaches, but circumstances occur in such a fashion that they do not get opportunities to display their true personality. Excellent psychoanalysizing and psychosynthesizing capability is seen that may excell them in the areas of psychology and counselling. They do not have to be proffessional to be an excellent judge of characters. They know how to use friends and others to the best possible together output. Combined values, resources and mixed assets are created very well which they cannot do by themselves. Thus, they will use others to build a good combines source of which they feel entitled to take a large share for themselves. Unexpected situations involving death, separations, legalities are noticed in their life, along with sudden help when they may need the most. They demand sacrifice from their friends because at one point or another friends have caused serious stresses to them. Independence or self-freedom is sacrificed for togetherness of opportunity. Somehow, they learn unusual lessons and experiences from their isolative/lonely period. However, they will try to hide their feelings and pretend as if nothing occurred drastically. Rebelliousness causes internal anxiety as they have some unreasonable internal phobias regarding such human behavior. Supression of hostilities, fear of isolation and uncertainity of the future, often seen here. Their reflexes, reactions, and objectivity need proper coordination. Inventiveness and innovation applied for regeneration or restructure can be quite important for this combination.

RETROGRADE NEPTUNE

In retrograde situations Neptune's qualities are more diffused, foggy, and uncertain. Instinctions tend to cover wider range than usual, but the focus might be less prominent. Idealism, vivid imagination and day dreaming can be seen in excess, creating stronger escapement needs from everyday life. Falling in love with the idea of love becomes significant. However, the native receives substantial shock when he comes to mundane reality. The boundary between the real and the unreal worlds is quite thick with a large region of uncertainties. Thus, the native is not confined to simple black and white situations, but he has to deal with substantial gray areas in between. This middle layer can be most unproductive in normal isolative sense. However, when in connection with either reality or true fantasy, most productiveness can be possible. Procrastination at the last minute decision making seen here. Strong creative potential seen in him, but he has to connect his creativity with either down-to-earth practicality or shear out of this world imagination. Fantasies can be very vivid and he has difficulty coming back to reality. Regarding spirituality, he is not so certain or sold on the usual ideas. This uncertainity is caused by the people in his environment who proclaim the path of spirituality that does not sound reasonable to him. It is hard for him to find a good spiritual teacher. However, after several frustrations he is ready to accept someone or many people as his spiritual guide.

His approach to true spirituality begins with deep material learnings. Thus, he evaluates his philosophical goals through the practical/material equations. He responds very unusually to confining situations. His first reaction is to fantasize and escape out of it. Then bring that knowledge and procedure to work out his reality. Here the native enjoys isolation, loneliness, but not the circumstantial confinement. The sense of free spirit is important even though his feet might be tied down. The native has a distorted sense of services as viewed from his spouse. Clash of idealisms can be noticed in partnership areas as the native often attracts people of much different goals compared to his own. It is also likely that this individual changes the hopes and goals all of a sudden bringing the clash as mentioned above. His instinct, gut feelings or psychic perceptions work very well for others, but he may not be able to count upon those instincts for himself. Wrong diagnosis, improper medication or abrupt reactions to drugs are likely in this case. Early morning dreams are most prominent here which can unfold various interesting areas around him with strange accuracy.

RETROGRADE NEPTUNE THROUGH THE HOUSES

Retrograde Neptune in the First House. Self disillusionment or lost self perspectives, instinctive, creative, artistic, talented & imaginative, blends with nature easily, fantasizes a lot, daydreaming, takes things for granted, knows without learning, gets high on himself, distorted idealism, repeats the same past life, escapement from pressures through fantasies, plans well but may not execute well. drifty attitudes, projects different personality, easily taken by charm, unusuality and make believe sensation, enjoys being lost.

Retrograde Neptune in the Second House. Artistic apprecation, creative values, financial fluctuations due to circumstances beyond control, distorted sense of money and possessions, almost a breakdown potential in mid-life period, secret dealings of resources, confusions, misunderstandings or deceit associated with personal values, idealism to the extreme in money management, spiritual assets but distorted perspectives, instincts become liabilities, inferiorities due to lack of progress in unworldly matters, color vision in focus, corrective eye sight, magnetic speech impact.

Retrograde Neptune in the Third House. Psychic sensitivity, easily influenced by the surroundings, learns through osmosis. mental attitudes foggy and uncommon, self confusions, fond of travel and imaginative places, make-believe relationships with brother/sister, easily intoxicated, clumsiness in motion, mental approach to spirituality or esoteric logic noticed, demands attention from others and then detaches from them, miscommunications or distorted truths, imbalanced learnings, unusual handwriting, adaptable & dramatizes nicely. Senile tendencies in the later years.

Retrograde Neptune in the Fourth House. Unusual family or make-believe happiness at home, escapement form home in search of vivid dreams, weak foundations, strong spiritual tradition in the family, distorted family unity, unique mother or her approach to life, gains through family inheritance but losses and deceits occur later in life, does not get what he truly deserves from the family, inactive parent appears much different than what it is, domestic confinements preferred, alcoholism at home, creative/talented display in the surroundings, lacks home discipline, fantasizes about glamorous home or living conditions, ghosts at home.

Retrograde Neptune in the Fifth House. Very romantic, creative, talented and imaginative, sense of being is very important than where and how he got it, daydreaming, takes things for granted in personal romances, fantasized romanticism, speculative losses or gets taken by schemes easily, adores children but may not have a large family. Confusion, separations, or deceits through children. Personal life can be distorted, disintegrated and inharmoneous, but the person will enjoy it on a different plane. Love and intoxication go together, a good giver of feelings and emotions, average grades in education except in the neptunian areas, loves to be in love with anything. Foggy.

Retrograde Neptune in the Sixth House. Changes in job due to vague interactions with coworkers, demands too much for his efforts, inefficient but uniquely creative. Hates monotony on the job. Insecurities projected constantly when he does not enjoy his work, strange weakness and abnormal health problems, distorted sense of work and services, deceives the unions or gets deceived through them. Uncertain work output, uncommon family structure on the mother's side of the family, institutionalized life in late years, wrong medical reactions, improper usage of drugs, medicine and alcohol, always expects a miracle.

Retrograde Neptune in the Seventh House Impressionable but projects wrong personality. Easily influenced by others, impersonal relationships and more than one situation fantasized. In love with an image rather than the person, socially oriented and expects reactions from others, dissilusionments in the partnerships creating potential deceits to and from it, music, art, talent, dancing, and sensational involvements important, dreams of an ideal situation without putting efforts to make it happen, public scandal or distorted opinions from others, influenced by magic, magnetism, and quick charm, always willing to help with remote motive.

Retrograde Neptune in the Eight House. Sexual fantasies, make-believe pleasurism, imaginative excess, spiritual assets gathered through others, confused sexuality or distorted pleasurism, fantasies and reality remain much far apart tearing the individual abruptly, it suddenly rains on his cloud nine, problems or sudden depletions in combined values/assets, mismanagement of other's resources, gets cheated by others or he is the ingradient in the mass deceit, miscommunication and eventual fog in personal sexual contacts, spiritual communication, mediumistic & psychic, knows other's motives by instincts. Death through over dosage.

Retrograde Neptune in the Ninth House. Unique philophies and beliefs of life, idealistic standards, fond of travel and distant places in real or imaginary situations. Confusions towards higher education or its usage. Misunderstood second marriage, does not listen to his own instincts. Psychic sensitivity from his family tradition, fond of people of different backgrounds and cultures, success away from home anticipated, widower, goals more important than the means. Ideas overtake substance, mystical inclinations, philosophical intoxications, legal problems.

Retrograde Neptune in the Tenth House. Changes in career due to variable attitudes, confused under pressure, weak father image or fantasizes about father figure, goals are very idealistic and he shoots high irrespective of their real execution. Considers himself creative, talented, and artistic, expects a lot of creative work opportunities, dreamer in his profession. Clash with in-laws, replaces a parent through marriage or partnership, social status expected, if not he assumes one, dual professions, deceits or misunderstandings from collegues, lack of ethics likely, neglects details and refuses to read between the lines.

Retrograde Neptune in the Eleventh House. Large group associations, considers himself friends to everyone, social invitations important, misunderstandings to and from friends, foggy attitude towards father's worth, may not get his fair share form him, mid-life crises hits him hard with many broken dreams, goals and hopes of life are highly optimistic but he insists on their realistic probability, offsprings or other's children suddenly cause problems in life. Fantasies in love received, gets involved with very unique groups, social butterfly, demands loyalty but does not get it from others.

Retrograde Neptune in the Twelveth House. Spiritual indulgence, expects things without efforts, fantasies are excessive, enjoys escapement from normal life. Lack of career and professions in later life, deceits from behind-the-scene actions. Institutional contacts or sudden confinements, past mistakes catch up with him. Strange family from father's side, unusual health problems to spouse likely. Esoteric growth nicely seen in this life due to uncommon suffering, enjoys isolations, learns through pure instincts, psychological ghosts in life, nervous emotional breakdowns.

RETROGRADE NEPTUNE RULING THE HOUSES

Retrograde Neptune Ruling the First House. Procrastination, lack of self-confidence and inner insecurities seen. Flexibility, adaptability and versatility can be noticed here which help the native in various areas of life. Compromising attitudes but verbal differences visible in him. His outwardly soft natured personality can be deceptive to others. Thus, he may be misunderstood or misjudged by other people. Willingness to give up his stand on certain issues makes him popular with friends, even though he does not have a circle of friendships. Work and marriage can be very significant areas of interests and exposure in his life. Pyschic perceptions, creativity, but cold objectivity seen in him. He demands a lot of attention and his touchy behavior is easily noticed. He is not sure of his creative talents but others convince him of the same. Daydreams, fantasies and quick runaway escapement tendencies seen here. Drinking, drugs or alcohol need attention as he forms habits very easily. Sympathy, apathy and sense of pity are important facets of his personality. Idealism and false goals need control for better life security in this case. The native has a lot to learn about his personality and needs to unfold his inner nature all through his life.

Retrograde Neptune Ruling the Second House Uncertainities and confusions regarding the financial areas are noticed here. Life values fluctuate or the native runs around in circles trying to identify his worth. Financial indecisions, procrastinations, and self-disillusionment can be seen here. He can be gullible and prone to deceptions from others. His instincts and psychic senstivity are excellent, but he underestimates their worth for practical purposes. His outlook for life is unusual, inventive, and experimenting type. A sense of exploration leaves him in the left field without serious practical achievements. Great ideas to make money can be seen, but the actual execution may be uncertain for him. Getting high on money and material things is easy but he can be most defracted individual when it comes to actually handling the resources. He places a great value on spirituality, pure love, idealism, and unworldly creativity. However, he may have a second thought regarding using them for his selfish, practical usage. Pennywise, pound foolish attitude can be significant here. However, regarding credit matters he can be slightly better off. On a fantasy, make believe or imaginary level he indulges in his values. Pleasurizing the resources or escaping from the materially oriented world causes inner confusions for him. His decision making regarding the financial area works best when he sleeps on it for a while. His spontaneous reactions do not always guide him truely. For that reason, he should avoid quick and drastic decisions.

Retrograde Neptune Ruling the Third House Although the native appears practical and stable outwardly, a lot of inner mental indecision and uncertainties seen in him. Inner nature can be much different than outward expressions. Learning through osmosis, instincts or symbology seen outwardly, but a lot of hard efforts are actually exerted here. Shy and sensitive attitude with an unusual way of expression seen. Feeling of misunderstandings or periodic deceit through brother/sister situations likely. It could be that the relationship never gets fully defined for the native to truly understand it. Mental flights of fantasies or creative ideas can be superb, but the native may not have good sense of practical applications. General mannerism is unusual and he may drift in and out of foggy situations. Good mind and mental process are possible here, but he is not sure of himself all the time. Unusual handwriting can be easily noticed as the native thinks one thing but writes another. This thinking and expression harmonizing takes time for him to achieve. Daydreaming or being lost in his own world can be observed here. He does not like to be alone but he can be very critical of the people in the surrounding environment. Imaginative, artistic, and creative writing or expressions very significant.

Retrograde Neptune Ruling the Fourth House Domestic activities and early childhood shows substantial diversification. However, the native is much too engaged in his own world of creative and imaginative fantasies to remember any of his early life. Relationship with mother can be fragile, uncertain and at times vaguely defined. Thus, both may exist together, communicate on a psychic level, but thay may still be quite far apart on psychological levels. The person is not sure of his position at home causing shaky roots of life. He is not certain where he should settle down. Should he follow the family tradition or open up his own branch of life away from every thing, becomes a serious issue for him. Family inheritance is there for the taking, but he is skeptical about it for no special reason. He can be just like his mother in many ways, but he wants to be different than that image. Domestic creativity, talented home applications, or industrious homey nature are very significant here. A sense of spirituality or communicative link with the family spirits seen here that is amazing. He enjoys entertaining at home where he can take different approaches or diversification to his sensational socializing. The home walls and boundaries provide him the means to fantasize and make-believe his imaginative goals. Some confusing issues, misunderstandings, or potential deceit regarding home, property or real estate areas need attention. Multiple changes in home and living conditions occur unexpectedly throughout life.

Retrograde Neptune Ruling the Fifth House Excellent creativity and applicable talent seen here. Romantic frustrations are converted into something practical and artistic. A sense of real pleasurism can be dreamed by this native. In love/romance, the native can be very gullible, idealistic, and very assuming in character. His anticipations and expected fantasies never come close to any reality bringing a surge of disappointment periodically. Often he is taken by the charm, magnetism and unreality of the other person and he seldom gets a chnace to evaluate the total interactions. As a child he needed a lot of attention but did not get it as expected. Subsequently, in further life he treats children very well based on past experience. He may not be very lucky in speculation as his calculated risks can be surrounded by cloudy circumstances. Pleasurism, indulgence and take it easy attitude can be very important to him during his early life. Taking things for granted or giving others the benefit of the doubt needs curbing in this case. He is like a butterfly in romantic pursuit or he would treat other people like that depending upon his mood. Sensation on a fantasy level overtakes his passionate intensity. Thus, he values feeling his love more than being in one.

Retrograde Neptune Ruling the Sixth House Confusions, misunderstandings and abrupt endings noticed in the areas of work and services. The native is very sensitive, imaginative, craetive, but touchy on the job. Thus, he does not like harsh competition or any strategic power play in it. His dealing with coworkers is on a sympathetic level and he expects calm and emotional supervisor. Often the superior will be like that who minds his own business. Subsequently, job progress hinders due to less ambitious boss above this person. The native functions very well on the job when he feels sympathy or sorry for somebody. Daydreaming, escapement from monotony and being industriously creative is significant in this case. He expects qucik progress without significant responsibility on the job. Health can be fairly average and fragile at times. Wrong diagnosis, improper diet, and allergic reactions to medicine are possible here. Liquid diet can be significant or a must for the native.

Complications or difficulties arise out of the mother's side of the family. When applicable, difficulty with servants, unions, workers, and their contracts. Possible deceit, theft or misunderstandings with them requires attention. Instincts on the job are strong, but not always productive or accurate.

Retrograde Neptune Ruling the Seventh House Very idealistic and romantic marriage ideas, noticed here. However, the other person's reality obstructs the native's fantasy creating potential misunderstandings. The spouse is taken for granted or the native expects adaptability from that person. The relationship may be based upon unreal foundation as far as the other person is concerned. In the eyes of the native, cloud-nine environment constantly exits in the interaction. Due to this mismatch, more than one marriage or several serious involvements noticed with a departing feeling of deceit. The native's objectivity can be cloudy or uncertain, frequently. As a result, he may not be the fair judge of characters. Problems with open enemies or he feels like others are jealous of him. He sees his dream in the other person and falls in love with that combination. He often needs to control the marriage or marriage hinges upon the financial worth of the together resources. Learning experiences through a partner that needs periodic freedom, escapement and fantasized existence. The native may not take that unrealistic route in life, but he gets stuck in the situation for a while. During the course of that existence, he experiences satisfied sensation.

Retrograde Neptune Ruling the Eighth House Sexual fantasies or exaggerated physical drive are consumed on a fantasy level. The relationship experiences spicy interactions and both parties need not have to be present simultaneously for it. Combined resources can be very significant in making and breaking the situation. Goals are unified to gather something of worth to both the parties, but the gathered material worth becomes the issue of conflicts. Phychic communication, spiritual exchange or mediumistic tendencies strongly present here. Some sudden reversals or complications arise out of combined resources, credit, group values, or insurance matters. Inheritance potential is strong, if one does not expect it. However all of a sudden strange set of circumstances will hinder in the actual division of resources. Fear of intoxication, heavy drugs or just the phobia of death seen here. Sensation overrides romanticism in this situation. Thus, the native wants to experience the full sensation than simply comprehend it on a verbal basis. Problems with sick people in the family, over dosage of drugs, alcohol, or fear of drowning are likely. Connections with corporations, institutions, or large established companies seen here; but frequently, the native gets disappointed with that structure and changes his close association or work to a smaller group.

Retrograde Neptune Ruling the Ninth House Strong interest seen in spirituality, metaphysics, and the universal understanding. Here the native procrastinates, reevaluates, and rebounds from his basic beliefs and philosophies in the hope of unlocking some life answers. His philosophies may appear shaky and uncertain at times, but his faith in the super god is strong. Things beyond his control he won't even worry about. Thus, an ability for blind faith in the high supremacy helps him minimize inner anxiety and worries for everyday life. Minor hassel or discontentment towards higher education seen. The native may even get disillusioned from that added knowledge as he cannot practically apply it successfully. Legalities, litigations, and even bad publicity potential seen in his life. When applicable, second marriage issue can be most confusing to him. His idealism and fantasy for out of this world such relationship crumbles under cold practicality. Distant relatives or success away from place of birth shows less promise than expected. This can be a good combination for philosophical, institutional, educational, or religious pursuits and administration. His individuality works better than combined efforts with another person. Travel can be important, but he is not very certain when he wants to.

Retrograde Neptune Ruling the Tenth House Career and professional changes are almost certain here due to drastic modifications of attitudes and increased needs for individuality. Grass looks greener in other areas of profession than his own. As a result, his quest for change and pursuit of that ideal rainbow brings several detours in career areas. He is very attracted and fascinated to new areas of applications. However, he cools-off and gets dischanted fairly easy once he experiences the reality. Freedom or independence on the job is very much needed and expected by him. He can perform best under his own supervision, as he needs time to fantasize and escape out of humdrum instantly. Vivid imagination, creative, talented applications of art, photography, music, acting, display or just make believe situations important in this case. Changes in career provide a sense of depth to his knowledge and creative wisdom. Difficulty with father or his spacy detached attitude towards the native cause psychological partition between the two. Many learning and relearning experiences are important through career, people of power, and authority and even bureaucracy in his life. Under pressure this native reacts very fuzzy, confused, and screemish. A sense of appeal just overflows out of him to minimize such squeeze from circumstances.

Retrograde Neptune Ruling the Eleventh House Quite affectionate and trustworthy attitude seen towards friends. Here the native takes them for granted in good and bad manners. There is a potential for mistrust, misunderstanding or deceit due to flexible arrangements, as far as others are concerned. Thus, friends do not come to help him when in need as the native labels wrong people under friendships. Larger group associations or nonselectivity of personal choices seen in this case. These interactions occur from all walks of life without specific goals of certain choices. Humanitarian, esoteric or universal treatment seen in general on a brotherhood basis. The native does not learn quickly any set-backs caused from his such attitudes and interactions as he enjoys this more than what it can do to him. Life goals and expectations are easy going type with periodic drifting tendencies. Aimless achievements or worry-free attitude about the future seen in him. The stigma for lack of direction comes from very possessive early family life. Often the native gets what he wants in early childhood, devoiding him for any self attainment. A sense of security is not important to him, but an effort to just live predominates his life. In general, low expectations seen from others by this native.

Retrograde Neptune Ruling the Twelveth House A strong sense of spiritual awareness and mystical affinity seen in him. No matter where he goes or what he achieves, his inner nature is guiding him on the path of spirituality. Inner doubts as to whether he would ever reach the state of universal consciousness threaten him periodically. He needs isolation to recouperate and get himself together. At times others see this as a self confinement. He has to keep himself busy in action when he is not alone. Once in his isloative mood, he achieves things on a mental level that gets programmed for physical execution. Alcoholic, intoxicating, or just getting "high" tendencies need attention. Habit forming nature is subjective to escapement indulgences. Hidden affairs, secrecy, or closet situations can be significant. Great inner phobias or psycholigical complexes visible in him. Often a shrink would have a great time with this native's inner workings. Psychic perceptions, mediumistic, clairvoyance, clairaudio tendencies can be worth noticing here. A bridge to the past and future can be easily accessible to this individual. As a result, relying upon some past life experiences can be seen at the times of needs. The native also unconsciously knows his future, but he may or may not make it happen consciously.

RETROGRADE NEPTUNE OPPOSITE MOON

Vivid imagination, perceptions, and sensitive feelings are seen here. However, the native has to put a lot of efforts to bring his dreams into reality. A sense of distorted reality is likely which causes the shifting of emotional perspectives. Emotional objectivity can be little distorted with touchy behavior and hyper moods possible. Withdrawn emotions take over any serious situations and escapement tendencies quickly arise as a result. Hidden problems or phobias towards domestication and life security are seen. Relationship with mother cannot be what it appears. Over compensations are done as a result of it to the next generation. Thus, one may overly mother the children or completely neglect them depending upon the reversal from his own early childhood interaction. Women in general are quite significant in this native's life. Dealing with femininity and learning from it is very important for his soul. It might be done in a total fantasy or in brave reality. Excellent emotional depth is seen, which can be very good for counselling others. However, this native can get too absorbed into others' problems or can create their problems as if they were his own. This subliminal trans-action can be a little bit dangerous and frustrating. A lot of Karmic fulfillment is done here or the native feels he is compensating for his recent past life. Reincarnation, soul travel, astroprojection, and vivid energy manifestations are quite possible and significant. Dealing with subjective reality is difficult for him. For this reason, he should take advice from others. However, he should be careful as to who gives him the advice. Intoxicating escapement tendencies are not the answers to existing problems, but imaginative, instinctive solutions can be the alternatives. Creativity when used with little practicality could bring this individual in excellent public focus. Life stability and establishing better foundations and roots are significant to this individual's growth in this life. All the creative, imaginative, and instinctive means are given to him to use on his road to life. However, he should not be indecisive, uncertain, and foggy about his gut feelings for the best outcome.

RETROGRADE NEPTUNE OPPOSITE SUN

Creativity provides good recognition in life. Short sightedness is seen here as far as the surrounding environment. Objectivity is likely to be foggy and uncertain. Individual goes after things irrespective of what others may say or think about it. Fantasy make-believe, and substitution help the native gain his own recognition and internal happiness. In reality, the person may not be aware of the true happiness as the outside world sees it. Confusions, sistortion, or misplaced interactions with father figure are likely. Any outside authority, pressure or dominance is dealt with through a runaway manner. Escapement tendencies provide the most joy and easy outlets in life. Sense of responsibility towards others is not very significant, but it is important to do things for the "self". Idealism is quite exceptional, but he takes things for granted. Life is full of rainbows here, but the native does not mind pursuing them with hard efforts. Temporary success in public life or high authority is noticed. However, he is prone to sudden deceit, deceptions, or scandle around him. Somehow, the environment is seldom as pure and holy as he expects. As a result, his idealogy boosts him up there, but it is also capable of bringing him down. Strong interests in creative, artistic, photographic, and make-believe projects are seen. A sense of display, perspective, coloration, and defraction of opportunities can be important. Outwardly, he shows great promise to others, but he has to learn to be consistent in his delivery. An uncertain and confused life in early childhood is likely due to the lack of proper perspectives and guidance. However, later in life he can be very successful once he learns about practicality and reality. In a woman's case, the male identity often gets distorted or they never measure up to her expectations. As a result of this, she gets confused and sacrificial or she becomes very independent and self sufficient. Dealing with intoxicants, or habit forming nature seen here. Social pressures create these needs rather than individual exploring attitude.

RETROGRADE NEPTUNE OPPOSITE MERCURY

Strong instincts and impressions are available but the native is forced to abide by the logic at the last minute. Sense of practicality prevails the perceptions. Gut feelings are given second priority compared to systematic synthesis. Details, precisions and methodology over take instant answers and quick recalls. Strain may be visibly created in most decision making as the native has to chose one side that is reasonably reliable by outside standards Creativity is often substituted by methodical mechanization. Ideas are excellent but are often tailored for practical usage. Absorbing capability intensifies the mind but the thoughts must precipitate and condense slowly. Thus, the mind may work fast inside taking into account feelings and judgments. However, outward acceptance of this thinking mechanism is not to its full capacity. Mind or mentality receives excellent priority in life in various areas. The native may have confused objectivity and the partnership communication can have a lot of kinks. Both may be on a super intelligence level but their ideas defract a lot. Communications, teachings, expression oriented areas are very significant in his life. A sense of service becomes strong for inner satisfactions. Escapement tendencies work very well within him in conjunction with good mental ideas as an outcome. Thus, when they withdraw, their experiences on an upper plane become the super ideas down here on earth. They are good with judgment of character for others. However, they cannot use that talent for their personal benefits most of the time. Psychic or paranormal communication, psychological evaluation needs, and deeper self-understanding are very significant here. Complex issues with confusion or fog regarding brother-sister relationships are quite possible. Stomach, digestive, or intestinal malfunctions are very easy as any suppressed stresses eat them up from within. Reflexes can be little unreal. Make belief acting, or simulations of others is quite prominent and easy for them. Doing and enjoying things on a mental level is very important and natural in this aspect. Substantial past life knowledge is available to them but they are hesitant to tap that source.

RETROGRADE NEPTUNE OPPOSITE VENUS

Excellent creative potential is bestowed upon this individual. However, he will only accept and adopt his superb talent for simplistic practical, and mundane usage. In a way, he likes to find an easy way out making him the lazy but successful artist.

Creativity here is quite subjective and he may not be a good judge or critic to evaluate others' work. Romantic fantasies are vivid and unreal at times. However, he is able to tell and depict the ones which provide him good pleasure rather than just the bummer type. Escapement tendencies are present here, but he may not use them in his love/romance department. Gentle, soft, and dreamy side of this personality attracts a lot of femininity to his life. However, many learning lessons and experiences through partnership are possible. Misunderstanding, disillusionment or just deceit may be noticed in his personal interactions. Reality and unreality pose a strong fight within him, but under most circumstances, reality wins at the end. Money and marriage are very important issues for this person. Aas a result, he may sacrifice many of his inner dreams and even deal with hidden unresolved issues for his ideal success in the areas of money, partership, and creativity. Hidden partnership or some behind-the-scene romances are very potential in real or fantrasizing manners. It is hard for him to understand the quality of emotional sensitivity coming from others. As a result, he over-compensates or under-estimates it. Dealing with women, femininity, theatrical, make-believe drama, art, music, and glamorous sensation is very important in this case. Purity of emotions are given the most priority as compared to anything else. As a reesult, he appears very pure, vulnerable, and ideal in nature. The idealism needs control from his side as it could be the dangerous downfall creating a drawback within himself. Sense of pleasure, habit formation, and indulgive excess at all levels can be well visible here. His idealogy can be the exact opposite to what he did in his prior life. Thus, he may want to conquer entirely different perspectives in this life.

RETROGRADE NEPTUNE OPPOSITE MARS

Fantasies are sacrificed for real action as the native prefers them in this condition. Inner impulses, instincts and gut feelings may not necessarily coincide with the actual actions taken by this person. Other people's motives appear foggy, vague, and uncertain making him much more self-confident about himself than usual. Hidden activities, past unfinished situations, or just subconscious are likely to hinder and bring blocks in his life goals. Sense of spirituality can be rejected for direct actions that are well visible. Anti-esoteric attitudes are likely to occur after one dwells into it with some frustrations. In a woman's chart it often distorts her perceptives towards males. This could begin right through childhood, relationship with father, etc. Magnetism, unusual forces of attractions, healings, manipulative psychological warefare, witch-craft, magic, etc., can be significant. Somehow, the native wants all the power he can get by whatever means available. He justifies this through misconception from others' reactions to him. Escapement tendencies and imaginative fantasies are present here, but he prefers live action rather than mental video to get the excitment. Dealing with hospitals, nursing, medicine, or pharmaceutical areas can be important to him. Improper medication, wrong reactions, chemical imbalance, internal body fire, fever, etc. are quite probable areas of concern. His involvement with the public may have some deceptive element or misconception. Strong mass appeal is noticed either way that seldom makes him quite isolative from others. War games, unusual strategies or just enjoying fantasizing warfare can be very important in his life. Physical energies are strong and at times he drives himself very hard to his objectives. However, his spiritual strength may not be up to his expectation or guiding him in an another direction. Thus, internal conflicts of spiritual direction and ego justification are likely. He can be his worst enemy as he has the power to suppress his spiritual guidance. He wants to take a chance in but on his own and not by some esoteric force. This way when he wins, it is not by the worldly prearranged situation but the power of his fist.

RETROGRADE NEPTUNE OPPOSITE JUPITER

An inner confusion as to what the life beliefs should be is noticed here. Sense of spirituality often gets sacrificed towards more conformed, standardized, or organized religion. Here the philosophies set forth by the society are more important than what the heart dictates towards the universal awareness. Social force towards the organized religion is so strong that the native has a difficult time within his own conscious. This turbulence often tears his fait in anything tangible. Institutional connections, oranizational approach and a high idealism are definitely seen in this individual. "Gut feelings" are compromised in order for him to accomplish something grand in life that is of worth to others. Fluctuating battles of these beliefs in life force the native in and out of his own confinements. Past life experiences, reincarnation, soul concepts, etc., are very prominent; but the native has limited access to them due to social pressure against such beliefs. Religious intoxication or submerged identity in basic beliefs cause many learning and relearning experiences. On a mundane level, the native can truly use his instincts, inner creativity, and psyhic perceptions to elevate himself in education, politics, religion, administration, or just to a comfortable high spot in life. Family cohesion, large grouping of family ties or excellent coordinating efforts on behalf of the elders are also seen here. Higher education will be easy but with mild hidden problems. Past issues often catch up with this individual due to his own psychological warfare, guilt feelings, or programmed phobias. Any sneaky or underhanded deals require very thorough preparation for him as he can punish himself more than what any organized society can do to him. Success through children or at least great expectations and fulfillments from them noticed. Better luck in legalities and good interactions with people of different cultural backgrounds noticed here. Great moral and social responsibility is undertaken by this native in the life time.

RETROGRADE NEPTUNE OPPOSITE SATURN

Practicality supersedes any imaginative and illogical approach. The native has a lot of inner feelings, instincts, and perceptions. However, he is not very certain of their reliability. As a result, he abides and follows the path of conventional tradition. Skepticism due to inner feelings of uncertainity is noticed here rather than from pure dogmatism. Family cohesion, dealing with strong respect towards elders and a sense of inherited tradition are very significant. Slow but steady progress occurs in life. Accepting responsibility at an earlier stage in life is quite possible. Previous life time can be very indulgive and irresponsible for this native. As a result, in this segment he is not likely to run away from responsibility, except for a better cause-purpose situation. Family orientation often dominates his views, thus making him sensitive towards "together" needs rather than his own progress in life alone. Careerwise, he can have good success later in life, especially during middle age and beyond. Some complex sacrifices done in career area as an investment so that he can benefit from it later. Thus, this individual may be forced to adapt under a supervisor or superior for a while but eventually he receives his rewards. In this situation, he has to keep his rebelliousness or hostilities suppressed. Creative ideas often get consumed within him, but their residual impact comes in handy later in life. Esoteric concepts and universal understanding are all within him, but his outward sense of rigidity takes time to accept it on a faith level.

Escapement tendencies, runaway attitudes, and fantasized idealism are created within him periodically. However, he is much too rigid and practical to give-up his goals or situations and detach suddenly. Tradition and going by the book is important to him as his faith in the "Karma of efforts" is quite strong. He does not mind hard efforts as he is prepared for set backs, periodically. In his pursuit of high ideals of narrow goals, he misses or neglects many imaginative, indulgive, and tempting dreams.

RETROGRADE NEPTUNE OPPOSITE URANUS

This generation often creates spiritual rebelliousness as they undergo strong needs to pull away from the standard concept of. spiritual religion. Somehow, the traditional beliefs do not answer their problems. A sense of innovative search for new consciousness is visible within them. Innovation and inventiveness on a real spectrum is very important than fantasy, substitution or make-believe satisfactions. Thus, they have to work hard to produce a product or real entity rather than get involved in the "spacy" imagination. Others do not always like and agree with their daredevil attitude or bold expedition. Freedom is valued by this generation but not in the form of escapement. They want real existance in an independent environment. Friendships can be a complex battle ground as most unresolved prior issues come back to hound them periodically. As a result, their friendships always have constant excitement, stimulation, and tension.

They are group oriented but in the form to create a small but powerful unification. Individuality will seldom be sacrificed in their group concepts. Unique and unusual means are very important foundations for their life pursuits. Logic of their decisions is very special and unique. They will compromise emotions, sensitivity and idealism for a unique but well planned logical approach. Sensations of realism are more important than imaginative substitutions in their personal life. As a result, they prefer short but many interactions rather than one drawn out situation with many compromises. Their hopes and goals appear to go in tangents as far as society is concerned. However, considering the path of mankind, it does not appear that way to the other generations. Creating a new pathway for future followers can be seen here, but it is in the form of scattered clues. As a result, time lapse is needed before people appreciate their efforts or progress in life.

RETROGRADE NEPTUNE OPPOSITE PLUTO

Spiritual and esoteric reforms are significant in this generation. Breaking away from older concepts of spirituality to create something new for the society to accept in the future is noticed here. Escapement tendencies, run-away attitudes, or withdrawal symptoms are looked down upon by them. Strength in true creation as a revival of a project has considerable meaning to this generation. Underhanded activities, under ground economy, basic subversive tendencies and low but deep profile associated with them. Foundations and structures for the sake of stability can be very important compared to what the creative display it can provide. Thus internal matters gain superiority over the external show or glamor. Hidden creativity is well applied towards internal beautification and the dreams have good foundations in this case. Alcohol-drug reforming tendencies or the people have excellent talent to quit the habits. It is true that they get the habit to start with before they can quit. However, this process of personal disintegration teaches them good lessons and experiences. Stripping away from the unnecessities becomes the goal of their new spiritual path. Underhanded or indirect means are utilized to combat deceptive situations. Thus, their means are no different than those of whom they oppose. Mass generation or mass destruction often occurs around this period. In an esoteric sense, soul orientation and redistribution is quite natural phenomenon of this time element.

RETROGRADE PLUTO

The retrogradation of Pluto is quite common in many cases. Pluto's generational impact brings a dualistic strategy in them. As a result, working with plans and counter-plans are very significant. This multitude of strategies is important as a fail-safe mechanism for them. Getting a pleasure out of creating a strategy is more important than its actual execution. Public opinion can be fairly divided in this case as the thinking process takes into account rebellious and anti-rebellious tendencies. An underdog appeal, at times, remains hidden for them. No matter what the chain of strategy can be, the last minute action may or may not coincide with the plan. Plutonian qualities enjoy a sense of penetration. Here due to retrograde phenomenon, the native will try to justify why he needs go under others skin. Justifying the detective logic has utmost importance to him. He can psychologically evaluate a person, but the findings remain unknown to him until he comes to a state of self explanation for its reason. This indirect evaluation of others helps him in many ways in terns of his objective opinions. The native enjoys instigation more than usual, but at the same time, he will avoid taking the credit for it. Combined resources may cause a clash of values. Thus, in his life time, he would learn the pros and cons of self worth and together values independently. The native may not want to be a front runner as he has a difficult time accepting the negative response from others. In political or bureaucratic situations, he can be best suited for power behind the scene. His advising capabilities can be much more helpful to others than to himself. For his calculated risks he often ensures himself against the worst possibilities. However, due to universal injustice, that special insurance policy can be his weakest design. As a result, when he is counting upon that last thread & support, he may not get it. For his best, he is better off never to need to use his ultimatum.

RETROGRADE PLUTO THROUGH THE HOUSES

Retrograde Pluto Through the First House. Magnetic and mysterious, self-conscious in an indirect way, strategist, goal orientation with methodology, energetic, temperamental and self-destructive, sex as a weapon used in the interaction, accepts challenges easily, clashes with own ideas, power hungry within limits, changeable personality and outlooks, burns bridges behind him, chances taken frequently, rebellious identity, very sociable and then quite withdrawn all of a sudden.

Retrograde Pluto Through the Second House. Enjoys money manipulation, does not like stagnant resources, takes chances in boosting self worth, sensuous demands, magnetic and appealing to the opposite sex, healing and hypnotizing capabilities, meddles in other's financial affairs, deep conscious reserve of feelings, easily hurt from comments, financial losses and gains teach him lessons, frequent .reevaluation of sexuality and its place in life, occult interest to help materialism, benefits through death, credits, and taxes, material indulgence and sensation to compensate actual romanticism.

Retrograde Pluto Through the Third House. Strategic thinking, critical, hypocracy, dual standards, enjoys game plans. Mental combat, argumentative, changes surrounding environment frequently, jealous of brothers/sisters due to circumstances, sudden travels needed for personal reliefs, destroys his own ideas in order to perfect them, sarcastic, means more important than goals, distorts the truth, mentally sadistic or cruelistic ideas, hidden complex bothers his mother for unknown reasons. Reads between the lines, enjoys challenging puzzles, mild mental kinks noticed.

Retrograde Pluto Through the Fourth House. Frequent domestic changes, enjoys loose roots of life. Insecure and uncomfortable at home, power play with mother or resents her domineering possessiveness. Rebellious childhood, mischievous early life, psychological or circumstantial gap from a parent, wants to know family roots and traditions, involves with domestic changes, construction, land, real estate and maintenance areas, benefits through many nonstandard areas of life, oil, gas, liquids, and underground barter, short recent past life gives him impatience to achieve things now.

Retrograde Pluto Through the Fifth House. Intense in love/romance, expects deep commitments from others. Takes chances without regard for consequences, problems with children or regarding having them, miscarriage, sexuality fluctuates in intensity, destroys romantic feelings to find their genuinity, trust and respect important in the situation, accepts sporty challenges but uses devious means to win, sour loser, unique way of study in school, noncompetitive on a larger group, one-to-one combat highly preferred, jealous, possessive and secretive in romance.

Retrograde Pluto Through the Sixth House. Strategy on the job, forms groups to combat other groups on the job. Difficulty with coworkers if they differ in opinions. Changes work frequently, weak health as he neglects the symptoms, holds grudges easily, but only for a short duration, problems with labor unions, abrupt and sudden collapse of life at the end, difficulty getting along with mother's side of the family. Worries about hidden activities or phobias in spouse's life. Confidentiality of work, work areas touch the masses or his efforts have a long term impact.

Retrograde Pluto Through the Seventh House. Attracts a powerful spouse, partnership enjoys constant stimulations, egos clash in marriage, spouse controls the relationship with strategy and the native allows it to happen, fights for justice, sensational rewards expected, highly influenced by masses or has the capability to turn them on, accepts challenges from open enemies but retreats quietly, resents others for their aggressions, more than one marriage or total restructure of the same, strong opinions but flexible objectivity. Love and sex cause many learning lessons in marriage, manipulative.

Retrograde Pluto Through the Eighth House. Complex personality, yields easily to others when he needs something. Intense passions but often sublimited through fantasies, possessive and secretly jealous, many serious relationships and complex turn ons, battle of wits in the partnership, combined values and assets pose good experiences, ability to deal with other's resources. Fear of death or being buried alive, psychological complexes eat him up from within causing periodic breakdown potentials. Sees death very closely or finds himself nearby when others depart.

Retrograde Pluto Through the Ninth House. Rebellious philosophies, goes against the family tradition, black sheep of the family, transitions from his beliefs to something different. Difficulties in higher education or nonapplications of it to practical value. Problematic second marriage or concern for its existence, bad publicity turns into benefits, enjoys people from different backgrounds and cultures, interested in politics, law and philosophy from critical view points, degenerate beliefs, faith in the strategy, disruptive end of the life, legal problems or litigations cause difficulties, revengeful when hurt.

Retrograde Pluto Through the Tenth House. Ambitious, authoritative, and self-trustworthy, expects too much out of father, creating father figure replacement in personal relationship. Recognizes authority but does not really respect it, revengeful under pressure, scattered and diffused tactics in competition, takes chances in life regarding career. Many career changes to achieve the objective. A sense of responsibility towards family tradition noticed but native finds his success away from home. Wins complete faith in the spouse only as an alternative to superiority, politics on the job or power play with coworkers, touchy sexual ego and physical drive sacrificed for ego fulfillment, superstitious.

Retrograde Pluto Through the Eleventh House. Changes in friendships frequently noticed, friendships used as stepping stones to success or friends end up using the person. Possessive feelings and unique love demanded. Underdog appeal in the group associations. Abrupt and major changes in profession in the middle of life. Undertakes difficult goals only to find frustrations in their achievements. Financial disagreements with father, interested in unique social

issues and how to combat them, helps others to be opportunistic, financial activities with friends and successive disagreements and disintegrated interactions.
Retrograde Pluto Through the Twelfth House. Complains behind the scene, supports the underdog, spiritual and mystical interests after major disruptions in life. Strange closet affairs or withholds many family secrets. Complex psychological profile, interests in penetrating other's motives, psycho-synthesis, psychodrama or psychological behavior studies, enjoys mysteries of life or life provides sensational unfolding of unique situations. Fear of old age, short previous life forces the native to achieve everything in early years, enjoys working on other's problems, counselling capabilities only when in the mood.

RETROGRADE PLUTO RULING THE HOUSES

Retrograde Pluto Ruling the First House. Personal strategies fluctuate and the native can become the victim of his own foul play. At one point he is very jealous, possessive, and intense. Then all of a sudden, he would change totally, leaving the other individual in the puzzle of darkness. The basic character, self-confidence, and self-assertiveness need to be much different than average forcing the native to create his own path in life. Once on his way, he compares his life with others with periodic repentance for his decisions. In reality, he would never be happy following the path of a normal personality. Thus, his unique way to achieve things is best suited for his personality. Strong love/hate combination seen towards others. Thus, he could hate a person he loves dearly and vice versa. He wants to be secretive but at the same time, he gives out enough information to reveal his character. There is a difficulty in subjective evaluation as he lacks the powers of self-reflection. When strategies backfire, he can be a sour loser instantly but recovers frequently. General complexity of personality seen here under the cover of simplicity.

Retrograde Pluto Ruling the Second House. Financial fluctuations and uncertainty of values seen here. The native has real large scale ideas to attain the financial security. However, he drastically changes his goals at some point in his life, leaving the earned empire unattended. Material possessiveness fluctuates as he has to learn mixed lessons from values and worths. His assets have a tendency to turn into liabilities. However, with his shrewd mind, he has the capability to convert liabilities into assets. When he has money, he appears poor; but when he pretends to be rich, it is usually at a time of depletive resources. This gives him a good gambling edge over others. However, he should not stretch his luck as the universal justice may not be with him. Excellent money-making ideas and strategies are possible with or without sufficient reasons for their execution. The native can turn his back on his financial commitments and simply walk away without guilt. Professional fluctuations or sudden changes in friendships can be connected with his variable material attitude. In a younger generation, this indicates uncertainties towards the spiritual values. Jealousy associated with materialism can be significant.

Retrograde Pluto Ruling the Third House Mental strategies, plans, and penetrating mind seen here. However, true purpose of their execution may remain hidden for the native. Not knowing why he is holding the grudge or the deeper reasons of hostilities may be invisible to him. He loves to get into mental combat, but he has difficulty untangling himself out of it. Very complex relationship with brothers/sisters noticed due to strange circumstances and early upbringing. A good mind is basically seen, but it can be susceptible to bad influences very quickly. Thus, the surrounding environment can easily afflict his mind with difficult habits. Learning through competition can be important. Thus, he has to test everything he learns in real life situations. Strange mannerism, critical attitude and negative outlook possible. Here the native often tests others as if enemy and then only he accepts some of them as friends. He would pick on people he likes but he can show his hostility with a smile on his face. Sarcasm is used as a tool to help others as the native can seldom behave straight forward. As the time goes on, he has to learn a great deal regarding his indecisions, insecurities, and fluctuating expressions.

Retrograde Pluto Ruling the Fourth House. The native is not certain regarding his roots of life. At times, he is proud of his tradition, family, and foundation. Then all of a sudden he resents being in that situation. Power play with mother can be easily seen through early childhood. Her possessiveness over the native can be untimely. Thus, when he wants it, he does not get it and vice versa. Sudden drastic changes in the home living conditions possible. Here the native may just pack up and up-root himself in order to establish a better life security somewhere else. His needs for life stability fluctuate from one extreme to another. Thus, at one point he wanders all over without regard for the future. Then all of a sudden he nails himself down for a long period. He greatly enjoys a part of his early upbringing but he is strongly hostile towards some other areas. It is hard for this individual to take the good with the bad. He would criticize the things that he treasures and gets pleasures from. Due to very short previous life time and abrupt ending of it, he feels he has been born in a wrong family at a wrong time period. As a result, he will try to adapt to the family tradition and structure in the beginning but rebel away from it later on. In many cases, exactly opposite situations of the above are noticed. The native's domestic security becomes or appears like confinement or true confinement may be seen as potential security in this case.

Retrograde Pluto Ruling the Fifth House. Quite interesting love/romance attitude seen here. Double standards are easily noticed or shown by the native. Thus, he wants to be possessive of the other, but he does not like to be possessed by the other person. This duality may extend in such a way that he wants to be possessed and be secured from others. However, he is unable to reciprocate that to others. As a result of this, many changes in romantic pursuits are possible. Once the native decides to settle down, he can do so at will. The power of his will may not be strong and long lasting. In a similar way his attitudes towards children and offspring fluctuate. He may or may not be sure what he wants out of that interaction and how he should go about it. Reversals in speculative luck can be seen. His best strategies or calculated risks can be the most simple ones. However, he cannot tolerate anything that simple, creating more eleborate plans which fail periodically. Not many hobbies are seen here. However, once he involves himself, he can be very intense in pursuing it. In his romanticism, he plays the guessing game. Thus, he expects romantic reciprocity without asking for it explicitly. Jealousy, sarcasm, and self-destructive tendencies need curtailment in that area for him.

Retrograde Pluto Ruling the Sixth House. Constant power play or sudden reversals in his atttitudes towards jobs and work area noticed. Thus, he fluctuates in his liking for the work he does. This changeability provides sensation and change of pace for him on the job. Mutual resentments, competitions, and inner jealousy are very significant with his coworkers. He will take responsibility just to prove others are not worthy of it, or he will watch with a grin on his face how someone fails in the same duty. He can be a good worker when he puts his mind to it. However, he enjoys scheming or planning more than actual work. He can accept dangerous challenges on the job as a part of his strategy. However, he will seldom carry out the true risk. On a physical level, actue illness can be noticed here. Wrong diagnosis or improper sysmtoms frequently seen. Some chronic family inherited physical weakness are often visible that the native should keep an eye on. The reaction to sickness can be very volatile here. Thus, he will go through serious situation as if nothing has happened. On the other hand, he would make a big deal out of some minor injury. Surgery or operations can be significant for the relief of his sickness when he least expects it. Excellent body healing capability noticed in him on a larger scale, but he would take a long time for some minor cuts and bruises on the surface.

Retrograde Pluto Ruling the Seventh House. Learning and relearning experiences from marriage and partnership seen here. Quite possibly more than one marriage or total restructure of the same one noticed in this case. Objectivity fluctuates and the native can respond unpredictably to others. In reality, the other people are the instigators for changes in his objectivity. Solitude is expected periodically cutting down on socializing. However, when he wants to truly socialize, others may leave him alone. His marriage partner can display competitiveness towards him. Thus, a struggle for control and superiority over each other is possible. Partnership provides a considerable chance for games in this case. Actually it is the spouse who triggers the game plan whether the native wants to play it or not. Subsequently, he has to participate in the interactions with or without his choice. As the cards lie, both enjoy the stimulation and sensational excitment. Here native's possessiveness and partner's jealous nature collide head on. The relationship is great as long as no shadow of outside interference comes into it. However, any origin of suspicion in the situation can be devastating to the relationship here.

Retrograde Pluto Ruling the Eighth House. Complex issues regarding the combined resources are possible. As long as the marriage or partnership is running smoothly, there is no major problem regarding the combined worth. However, common resources can be a volatile region to provoke the problems to worst limit. The sexuality can be very intense, jealous, and possive. However, sexual cool-off can occur instantly leaving the relationship icy cold abruptly. As a result, both parties have to adjust to this periodic hot and cold region in order to maintain a good long term relationship. The native has much different sexual fantasies than what he enjoys in real situation. He encounters minor problems of adjustment when he transitions from fantasies to reality and vice versa. Some problems with credit matters, inheritance, insurance claims, etc. likely due to circumstances beyond control. The native has a lot to hide in life or he feels the need to keep substantial parts of his personality undercover. However, at times he has difficulty locating what and where he hid it. Strong interest in the occult, metaphysics, or mysteries of life seen in this case; but he may not be certain as to how he can benefit from it all. Life after death, reincarnation, or deathology can be significant to him. Excellent powers of penetration, psychoanalysis, and evaluation techniques are seen. However, he has difficulty trusting his own subconscious.

Retrograde Pluto Ruling the Ninth House. Complete change over in philosophies and life beliefs seen in this case. It occurs not by choice but due to surrounding influences. A great need to experiment with one's own philosophies seen with an outcome of new revelation of life. Even though the native is uncertain towards higher knowledge and its pursuit, it occurs unexpectedly enlightening him with the universal exposure. Passionate attractions towards people of different background and culture can be noticed. However, the native comes to a crossroad where he has strong negative feelings about the same. Legalities, litigations, and delays in higher education noticed here. Abrupt reversals in the legal matters likely in the form of counter charges or being sued by the party the native wants to go after. Institutional or bureaucratic delays are most significant here but the native overcomes them with strategy of his own. In doing so, he walks a very thin line around the legal boundary. When applicable, second marriage issue causes complications almost as bad as the first one. The native has a deep urge to withdraw and run away to a strange place. However, once he accomplishes that, he cannot wait to come back or go someplace else. Thus, he enjoys travel rather than relocation.

Retrograde Pluto Ruling the Tenth House. The native is quite good at manipulating his needs in his career areas. He learns since childhood the use of fluctuating ego for the best outcome. Thus, his flexible ego can take the form to fit the needs. The opportunistic nature or strategy for such opportunities are his good assets. Power play with father or key male identify seen here. A need to compete with that father image or at times "do better than him" attitude gives the native considerable driving force. In resolving the ego clash with such authority in life, the native has to combat a lot of frustrations and even swallow his own pride periodically. In career, he enjoys strong ups and downs along with the calculated risks. Thus he is willing to fall down in the hope of climbing higher than an average person. He is best suited for a number two person in the organization as psychologically, he may not be able to withstand the pressure of being the top authority. In political areas, he can become the victim of mass outrage or his own strategy kills him. If he fails to watch his steps, his supporting rope can hang him in strange circumstances. He can be very proud of his heritage but for a much different reason than he should. A strong woman's support helps him achieve his career status. However, his power hunger creates the problems in the same personal relationship.

Retrograde Pluto Ruling the Eleventh House. Friends are often manipulated here or the native becomes the victim of their manipulation. Consequently, many changes occur in friendships. Here today gone tomorrow syndrome seen in the friendship classification of this native. The person is often forced to change his hopes and goals due to changes in his surrounding environment. The corrected goals do not always please him, but eventually, futuristic reality makes him happy. He can be quite possessive of his friends but the friendships get in the way of his true romantic interactions. Subsequently, friends are compromised for betterment in personal interactions. In his group associations, he can have a different voice than others. At the least he expects different treatment in that grouping and he is willing to pay its price. Social sensation is important to him but his friends can be jealous of his accomplishments. A lot of love is expected from others by this native but not really gotten. Some complex issues arise out of inheritance from father's side. Quite likely, doing things against his father's wishes leaves him with financial lack of compensation from his father.

Retrograde Pluto Ruling the Twelfth House. Here the native is not certain of his past life accomplishments, as a result, he tries to repeat his achievements. In a previous life, he lacked a sense of responsibility. Unconsciously, he still has that with him. However, periodically, he gets the urge to prove himsilf in the outside world. In many cases, his laziness gets rewarded in terms of added comforts. Thus, his need to be self-sufficient and worthy of himself fall short of expectations. He often counts upon the rewards from the past, but his past account may not be in active position to help him. Working in isolation or behind-the-scene can be important for this person's destiny. Sometimes, he understands his motives and subconsious very well but he has the power to confuse himself with his eleborate decisions. Sexual fantasies are so strong in here, the native has difficulty finding equally pleasurable reality. Occult interests, spirituality, life after death, etc., are significant parts of his search in life. The reasoning power is excellent but he has to work his philosophies in isolation. He gets tired of his isolation and self-withdrawal, but they can be his major learning lessons. Spiritual growth is necessary and it is achieved with or without his willful participaton. He is rewarded for his crimes with an opportunity to do something nice in this life.

RETROGRADE PLUTO OPPOSITE MOON

Learning and relearning experiences often seen in this case due to women, femininity, and emotions. Emotions are very vulnerable and the individual will do any thing within limits to achieve that objective. Here the personal sensitivity overrides all other strategies in life. Emotions are quite excitable and explosive. Psychological restructure definitely needed in order to achieve a better life foundation. In earlier childhood, mother, home, and nearby environment dominates the native, but the circumstances often bring disruptive situations. Thus, motherliness and women in general are important in bringing life stability to him but at the same time they become the source of problems as well. One has to learn this complex dilemma while still remaining in the same environment. Separations from a key woman are brought out due to circumstances just to check one's learning ability and eventual capability. Combined values are secondary compared to one's own life stability. As a result, the native may give-up partnership status, if his own roots of life are at stake. Response to emotional matters is very fast and quick. Thus, emotional manipulation becomes a viable part of this native in one way or another. Individual view points are often forced to diffuse to justify the public needs. As a result, dealing with people, mostly women, becomes an important tool in his life growth. Psychic and occult communication with the long line of family spirits possible. Here the tradition, family foundations and personal integrity are so strong that no family spirit would dare separate from this individual. Inheritance from mother or her side of the family is quite likely. Imbalanced nutrition or improper food assimilation is likely here. Chest, mammary glands and hormone imbalance need periodic attention in this aspect.

RETROGRADE PLUTO OPPOSITE SUN

Rebellious attitude often provided by this aspect of opposition is much less here due to retrogradation. As a result, rebelliousness in general is towards a specific authority. A sense of respect and authority is shown by them as long as an outside leadership is well visible. Respecting an authority in the hope of being an authority some day is quite likely. Tensions with father or male dominance noticed, but the stresses are often internally consumed and justified. Revenge becomes a goal rather than an intermediate play. Success, recognition, and power are achieved by any and all means. In its execution, he finds many challenges and overcomes most of them. Tendencies to resent the masses are often noticed, as the subversive means are loved more by him than the identities. Reactions to public criticism are sarcastic but well controlled. An ability to find one's own external focus and demand for a spot light from others seen in this case. Combined sacrifices are done for individual recognition. Sexuality and hidden motives are suppressed for the sake of pure and sensitive outside image. Inner inhibitions are often kept well hidden from others by this native. Circumstantial separation or just psychological gap is noticed between father and the native. Downfall often arises in his life due to insufficiently buried past matters. If one can face the past in a constructive manner, this aspect will bring excellent rise in life. Success in later life quite likely whether it is from good or bad publicity. Sexuality is often compromised by him for better romance and idealistic pleasures. Children receive higher priority in life compared to one's own sensational needs. Speculative luck is possible for this native, but he often sacrifices combined values and others' resources for it. Occult creativity can be significant but the native has to create a mystic in his creative output. Inheritance is often left to the children rather than to the spouse in this case.

RETROGRADE PLUTO OPPOSITE MERCURY

Here logic behind any strategy is highly important. The presentation, communication, or expression of what to do is more important than the actual undertaking. Thus, barking is more crucial than the bite. Pluto in this case has to give priority to the Mercurial function. Logic and details thus become crucial factors for him, no matter what the game can be. Mental manipulations highly significant at the cost of draining of mutual reserves of energy. Inward depletion of energy in this case creates excessive communicative needs or a nervous disfunction. Brother/sister relationship(s) are very important foundation for his psychological growth. The native may play a lot of mind games within the nearby environment. Mannerism is pleasant but there is substantial withholding of 'devilishness.' Good success on the job noticed here as his shrewd mind is always a step ahead of others as far as any company politics. Forceful learning is noticed in earlier life. The native wants to know why he is learning in spite of whatever the topic may be. His mental combat is subjective and seldom it will be used to rescue others from a verbal battle. Minor accident prone tendencies in travel are likely. Mental attitude can be highly taken regarding sexuality and any occult matters. Whenever possible, he loves to drain others on a mental level and at times he would even challenge others of their capabilities. Good detective tendencies properly cultivated in this case by the native. Quite peculiar attitudes regarding other's resources may be seen here. The native has to deal with other's resources whether material or esoteric in quality. A sense of responsibility is often undertaken, when others fail to achieve the objective. Thus, he takes it upon himself the burden, others have refused, rejected, or tossed away. Learning/relearning lessons from inheritance, credit, taxes, or group values definitely likely in his life. Unusual speech pattern is likely, such as too fast or too slow in expression.

RETROGRADE PLUTO OPPOSITE VENUS
Subjective goals and objective desires often create tense situations in his love/romances. High inner idealogy and pure love often get corrupted due to outside environment. Power play in personal relationship becomes a necessity rather than an unavoidable fact. In spite of this, true love wins most of the time. Love is given considerable priority over sexuality and sensation. Feelings, inner comforts and the right music of the soul still fight a winning battle over the jealousy, practical possessiveness, and sexual kinks. Self worth becomes more important than huge combined resources. Emotional prostitution can be slightly visible in the situation but the native seldom becomes its victim. Partnership is considered precious entity rather than what it can bring him individually . Ideality overtakes the greed, to conquer things together. Tensions with women can be significant, and at times become grave learning tools for him. Here any and all strategies are allowed as long as they are used for the pursuit of the true love. Love/money, and sex get entangled with complexity that the native eventually gives up upon their unique ideal combination. There is quite often an uncontrollable cash flow situation — too little or too much resources. Charm, magnetism, and politeness are excellent plus points to this personality but outside influences force him to misuse them. Personal sensitivity and partnership stability are quickly triggered by outside hostility. The lesson to learn is to control emotions, feelings, and accept the limits of self sex appeal. Strong perceptions and penetrating mind seen here, but the native cannot use it to probe his spouse on a deeper level. Here the person has to set aside this special talent as far as partnership interactions are concerned. Outside that situation, he can be very well informed of other's deeper motives. Some complications are possible regarding any inheritance coming from the spouse's family.

RETROGRADE PLUTO OPPOSITE MARS
Individual actions and activities are of prime significance and the actual means to achieve them are secondary. A touch of ruthless character seen here, but the native is forced to be so due to others around him. Power play, physical activities, and considerable highs and lows of energy are noticed. Violence from others affects this individual and as the time goes on, he is forced to adapt to the disruptive environment. Getting high on the force and utilizing the macho character are important. Individual projects/goals and activities are significant as compared to doing the things on a grand scale. As a result, he prefers individual, one-to-one com-

petition rather than team oriented activity. Subjective sneakiness or tactics which only work for himself are seen. Thus, his strategy may not work for others. Sexuality is sacrificed for other subjective achievements. Thus, direct energy applications or their visibility are more important than showing one's strength of libido. Self becomes more tuned in as compared to his place in a partnership. He can draw from combined energies to boost himself in the environment. This aspect is more prominent in a male chart for self boost than it is in a female chart. In a female chart, it often indicates a need for a "hen-pecked" husband or someone who can support her life goals significantly. Accident prone tendencies are visible in this retrogradation, but due to outside surroundings rather than his own actions. Learning through other's strategy or being able to adapt their's to his own mind is important for this individual. True power is given the superiority over the power of the will. Thus, the strength has to be a proven factor for him, than just a strategic threat. Impatience needs control here as the person gets tired of the waiting game. The actions and force are often displayed due to irrational and impatient behavior rather than backfired strategy. Here the fist moves faster than any elaborate plans.

RETROGRADE PLUTO OPPOSITE JUPITER

Personal philosophies and basic life beliefs remain the pivot points around which the individual keeps his strategies and plans. Goals often remain unaltered but the methodology changes depending upon the circumstances. The person gets into the habit of looking within to achieve things around him. This internalizing focus guides him nicely on his path in the esoteric walk. He often abides by the standards, restrictions, and law even though within himself he enjoys rebellious strategies. What he could have done and could have accomplished makes him more happy than just breaking any standard routine situation. He often sticks to his culture, basic philosophical format and upbringing, even though others around him come from wide range of samples. Outward faith is significantly dominant as compared to inner gut feelings. Hidden phobias bother him, but he will still walk on the same straight line. On a physiological level, it may create glandular malfunctions and many crucial changes occur when biological fluctions are seen in life such as puberty, change of life, etc. On an institutional level a lot of politics occurs behind him, but his faith will carry him through most rough situations. Spiritual values, are more important than mundane material resources or sexual indulgences. Partnership for him involves greatest merging of the souls and philosophies rather than anything else. Success in politics, international activities, and legalities will be seen but with greater compulsion exerted on him from others to be there rather than his inner drive. Faith gains superiority over the fist in this case. Idealism can be much more important to him than any subversive strategy. In certain cases, second marriage can be given greater priority over the combined values of the first situation. Thus, he sacrifices his together worth in pursuit of his idealistic dream mate, the second time around. Financial success can be visible here over and beyond the calculated risks taken to achieve it. The native is very self conscious of his publicity and he will do everything to keep it intact.

RETROGRADE PLUTO OPPOSITE SATURN

Inhibitions, orthodox, old fashioned ideas suppress considerable inner dilemmas. Strong respect, trust, and willingness towards the authority diffuses internal rebelliousness periodically. As a result, the individual builds considerable resentments within, over a period of time, towards the social structure. However, his ability to respect the authority and sense of justice force him to reevaluate his stands towards others. Father figure, family authority or just the pressure from conventionality provides a guiding direction to this individual. Strategy and game plans have to abide by rules and regulations in general. This creates a person who can manipulate very well within the legal, moral and social boundaries. A sense of structure, discipline and persistence is embedded within him since early growth. A need to run away from family is likely but the obedient side keeps the person from making drastic decisions. Clash with father or authority often seen but he goes by their wishes eventually. This aspect often creates a rebellious or slightly antisocial generation, but they still need a strong leader whom they can abide and respect very well. Confinement for the sake of freedom seen here. Thus, they may create self limiting situations in order to evolve themselves out of existing circumstances. The native's father often undergoes a considerable change in friendships. Quite likely his friends disappear abruptly or the social status gets depleted unexpectedly. This sudden shift in the father's life affects the interaction with the native. Due to changes in father's sudden hopes and goals of life, the native has to learn to achieve things on his own. As a result, internal ambition building seen through fairly early in life. Some complex issues arise out of family inheritance or family wealth. Here the person might be individually isolated from what he rightfully deserves. At times all he gets is the tradition, responsibility, and family burden without proper material rewards. In politics, government or bureaucracy the native can be successful as he knows how to manipulate circumstances and overcome rigid barriers.

RETROGRADE PLUTO OPPOSITE URANUS

Quite an unusual, unique and independent generation occurs with this aspect. Goals are created, constructed and executed for the sake of better individual and group freedom. Independence and unique pursuits are achieved with whatever means possible. Regeneration created with sacrifice for better humanity. This humanitarian orientation forces group compromises, in order that some section of the society gets elevated. Investing in future has more meaning here than living in the present. Collection of unusual talents to build a better together perspective noticed here. Innovative outcome is aimed at by using repeated and even frustrative efforts. Inventions which occur here are simply relabelled older products or concepts. Goals may be excellent, but the inner crucification loses substantial efficiency of achievement in this case. Improper and non-optional usage of resources possible here to achieve what somebody else may want someday. Others are sacrificed to please a third party in this case. Friendships are preserved at the cost of demolition of the self empire, simply due to unique principle. This generation becomes very important part of the history as a stepping stone for the forthcoming civilization. Quite stubborn and fixed attitudes are displayed in this generation. Unique persistence and objectives seen towards the financial future of the community. Sensation may be compromised for independence and freedom. Here the security remains well within the native but not properly expressed as one of the prime needs. Unusual sexual ideas are often suppressed in this case. The social pressure can be strong enough so that the native would not want to reveal his view points towards sexuality and the freedom of libido. Psychic communication, intuitive feelings from beyond or idea transfer from the deceased are likely. This generation often begins a jigsaw puzzle of life but leaves it unfinished for the future generation to complete.

Our Recent Publications

RETROGRADES $6.95
The retrogrades as an opposition phenomenon. Various combinations of retrogrades with indepth meanings. Retrogrades in the houses and ruling the houses. Retrogrades in various astrological applications.

ASPECTS MAGNIFIED $4.95
All major, minor and many unknown aspects delineated. How to use the apsect in a wider chart analyses is included. Over forty different aspects are studied in this text.

LUNAR NODES $5.95
Understanding the concept of Lunar Nodes through your Karmic Controls. Natal and progressed aspects to Nodes. Transiting Nodes in the chart. Karmic compatibilities.

DEGREES OF THE ZODIAC MAGNIFIED $7.95
Each degree contains a zodiac within. Degree meanings derived using the concept of magnification. You have to test it yourself to believe it. 208 Pages.

PRECISE PROGRESSED CHARTS $5.95
If you can set up a natal chart, this book will help you in predictive delineations method based upon generalized secondary progressions. The EVENT formation is well explained by these charts. 110 Pages

MOON MANSIONS $5.95
The concept of 27 Moon Mansions is used here to synthesize the chart rather than our usual twelve zodiacal signs. The planets in each of the 27 mansions are described in this text. 92 Pages

CARMIE AND THE OTHER WORLD (POETRY) $2.95

Mohan Enterprises
P.O. Box 18334
Roch., N.Y. 14618